Against the Structural Weight of Catastrophe: A Poetics of Negation

Laura al—Tibi
& Amr Amer

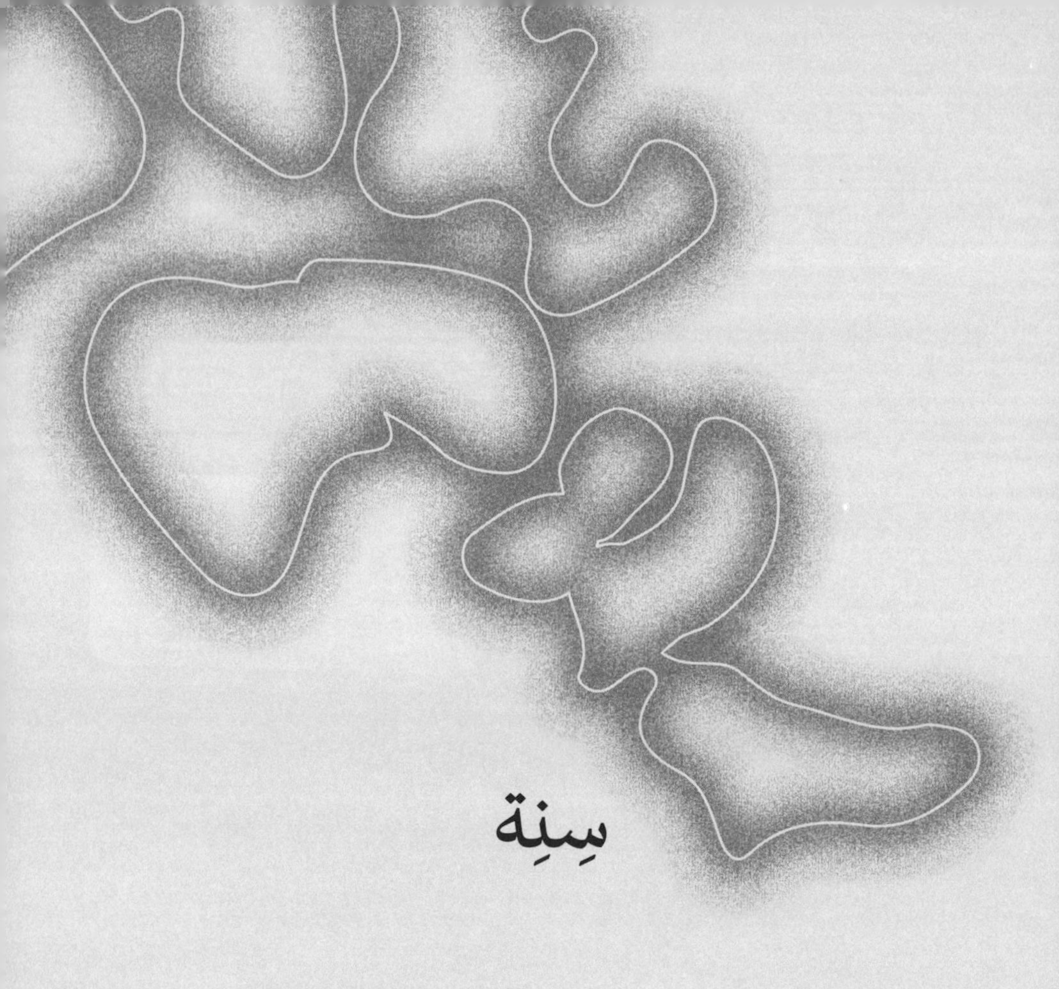

سِنِة

هذا

إلي

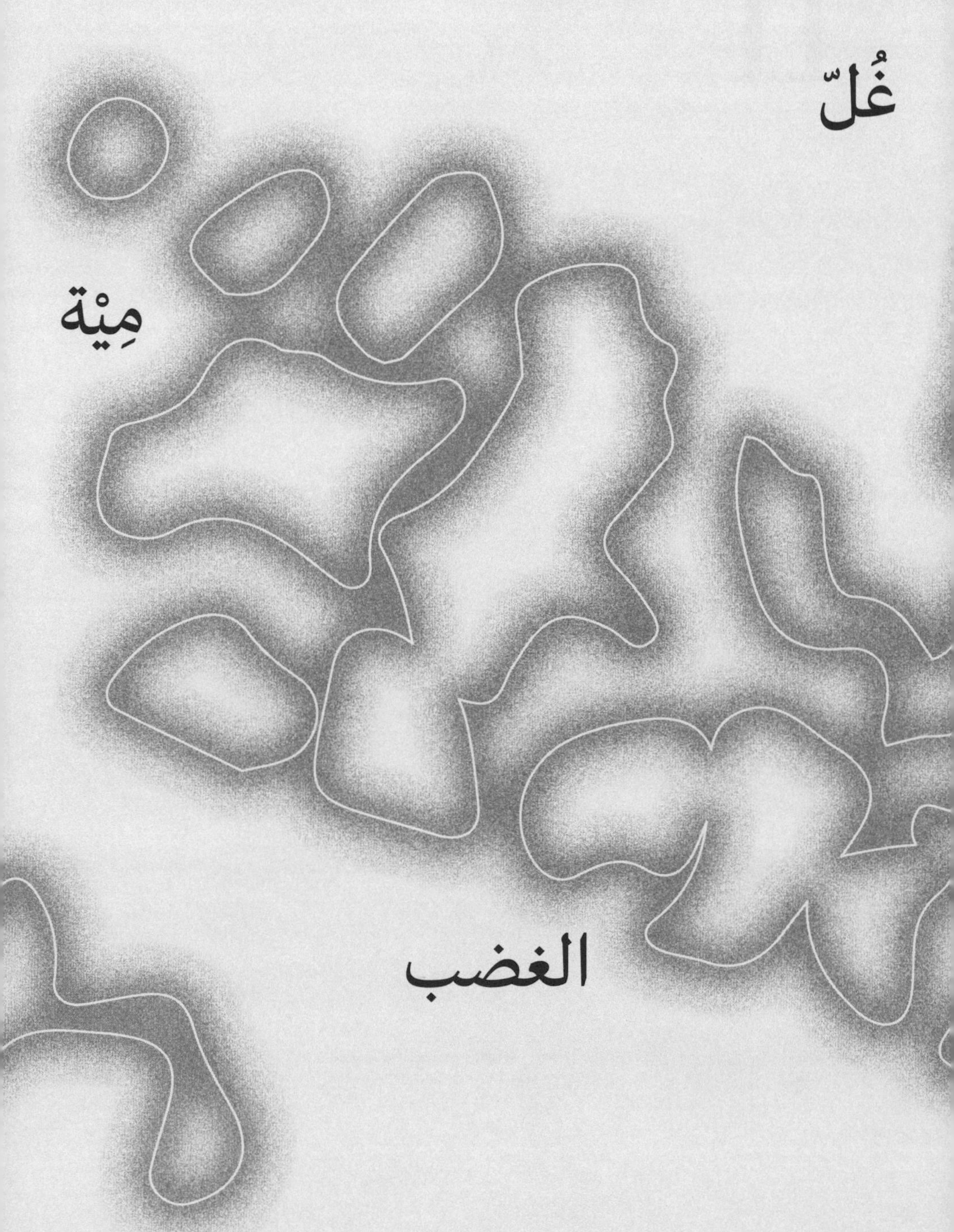
غُلّ
مِيْة
الغضب

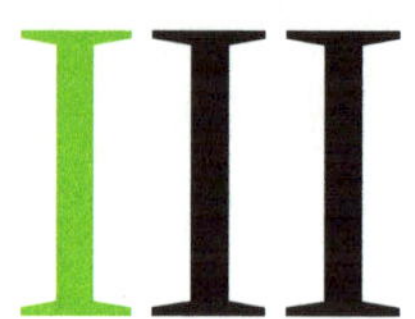

What does it mean for a land to be severed from its surroundings, its ecosystem cyclically shorn until it is stripped down to "bare life"? And its people, what becomes of them? Expelled, dislocated, decimated. What conditions their reunion with the land, their imperative to return and resow?

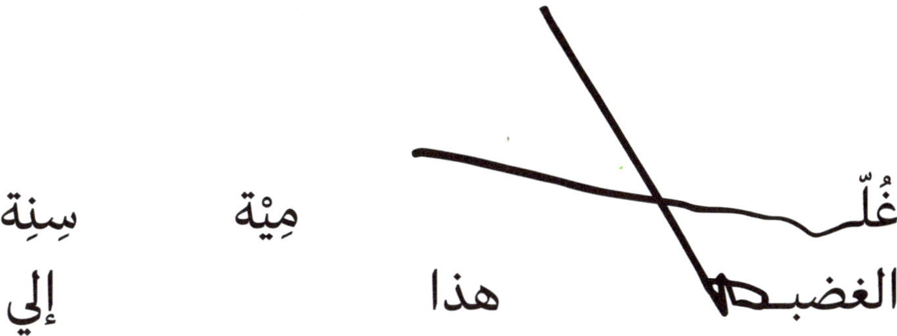

We read the Palestinian Catastrophe as a series of negations, the aggregate of which is an absence horded on hewn land. It is the discursive and physical emptying of Palestine, the disavowal of our bond with the land, the razing of our harvests, the ruination of our homes, and the suspension of our traditions and rituals, so deeply attuned to the cadence of the land. While the land has been slowly eroding for over a century, 1948 marks a calamitous loss, birthing the Catastrophe and our ensuing affliction. "And how can I but call it a Catastrophe [*Nakba*]?" writes Palestinian historian ʻArif al-ʻArif in the introduction to his 1956 opus on the Nakba, "for we have been catastrophe-d [*wa qad nukibnā*]."[1] The Nakba, as Palestinians have explained, is not a single event but an ongoing structure for which European colonialism is the ideological progenitor and Zionism—unexceptional and strikingly derivative—its most callous executor. Catastrophe cannot be weighed down or compartmentalized. It permeates the land and fills the body, spilling out against the structural weight of colonialism in refusal. What form might the enormity of Catastrophe take, and by which political grammars?

1
ʻArif al-ʻArif, al-Nakbah: *Nakbat Bayt al-Maqdis wa-al-Firdaws al-Mafqūd, 1947–1949*, vol. 1 (Sidon, Lebanon: Manshūrāt al-Maktabah Al-ʻAsriyyah Lil-Tiba ah wa al-Nashr, 1956), 3, as translated and quoted in Joseph Massad's "The Cultural Work of Recovering Palestine," *boundary* 2 42, no. 4 (2015): 190–191. See in particular Massad's differentiation between the English word "catastrophe," with its Greek etymology meaning "a sudden turn," often used in the more passive context of natural disasters or cosmological misalignment, and the Arabic term "Nakba," which describes a catastrophe brought on by Zionist settler-colonialism that subsequently produced Palestinians as "*mankūbīn*," or a "catastrophe-d" people.

اتْبَرّا من أبوه عالعَلَن
سَلَخوا بعض غمزة تمثيل
شجر جوّا العُش فاجأهم
"كيف ما كفّاكم تنكيل؟"
ما العُش مِش عُش
العُش هاد منجم
قَسّى جيل وَرا جيل وَرا جيل

In their ongoing body of work *May amnesia never kiss us on the mouth*, Basel Abbas and Ruanne Abou-Rahme theorize the negative in affective terms, introducing it as an aesthetic and political category that emerges from the land—not just as the site of dispossession, but as a generative body sprouting indigenous life in the face of repeated destruction. Their practice immerses us in the land through an embodied filmmaking—sinking into the soil, moving with the vegetation, and breathing through "the pores of this sea and land they called dead."[2] Beneath the layers of colonial rot lies an animacy ringing through millenia as it binds the ancestral dead to the living. This process of becoming allows space to unfurl, releasing caged breath and, with it, room for an otherwise. The duo's theorization of the negative in the Palestinian context offers a framework from which to read Catastrophe not just as an ongoing structure, but as something that unfixes, unearths, tunnels and mutates, coming apart and together again.

However, before we turn to this otherwise, we first need to confront the structural density of Catastrophe and attend to the violence of its operative negation. At the formal level, Zionism negates and "disappears" Palestinians, generalizing us into Arabs, able to float into any neighboring nation, and not Palestinians with millenia-old ties to the land. Its violence shifts between tenses, distorting history and suppressing a past that continues to elicit renewed

2
Basel Abbas and Ruanne Abou-Rahme, *May amnesia never kiss us on the mouth*, 2021–, https://mayamnesia.com/.

shock with each uncovered episode. Our removal and subsequent invisibility demand archival redemption, a scramble for the evidential power of the past to prove that Palestinians have always existed. Photographs, land deeds, "Mandatory" passports, and other bourgeois accouterments of modernity are summoned as we exclaim, "Look→ we were once modern!"[3] and therefore worthy of visibility. However, evidentiary claims are consolidated through institutional power and its regime of truth, which mediates the "having been there" of Palestinians as having ***not*** been a citizen of this nationless "there."[4] One's attachment to the land becomes redefined through a nation-state framework of belonging measured through citizenship, dangerously conflating statehood with liberation.[5]

3
Oraib Toukan, *Sundry Modernism: Materials for a Study of Palestinian Modernism* (Berlin: Sternberg Press, 2017), 30.

4
This is precisely the sentiment expressed in Golda Meir's oft-cited statement: "There were no such thing as Palestinians. When was there an independent Palestinian people with a Palestinian state? It was either southern Syria before the First World War, and then it was a Palestine including Jordan. It was not as though there was a Palestinian people in Palestine considering itself as a Palestinian people and we came and threw them out and took their country away from them. They did not exist." Frank Giles, "Golda Meir: 'Who Can Blame Israel?'" *Sunday Times*, June 15, 1969.

5
Or, as with the Oslo Accords, compromises the latter for the former.

شو دَرّى سماواتنا
هَيْ فتافيت مَحّاي
هَي غطاية مجاري
هَي فِطرة غُنّاي
شو دَرّى سماواتنا
الإثبات مَضْيَعَة
التّصحيح غَلَط
غلَطة مْقَطَّعة
شو دَرّى سماواتنا

The quintessential image of our absented presence is not the title deed, the historical photograph, or the identity card, but the land itself. Razed and ruined, it testifies to our Catastrophe and buried histories. It indexes not just our trace, but the sisyphean attempt to efface it. How does one represent land, let alone its loss? When it is fragmented and hollowed out, where does its history go? This image of loss, of absented presence and Catastrophe has been distilled into a portrait ***in the negative***:

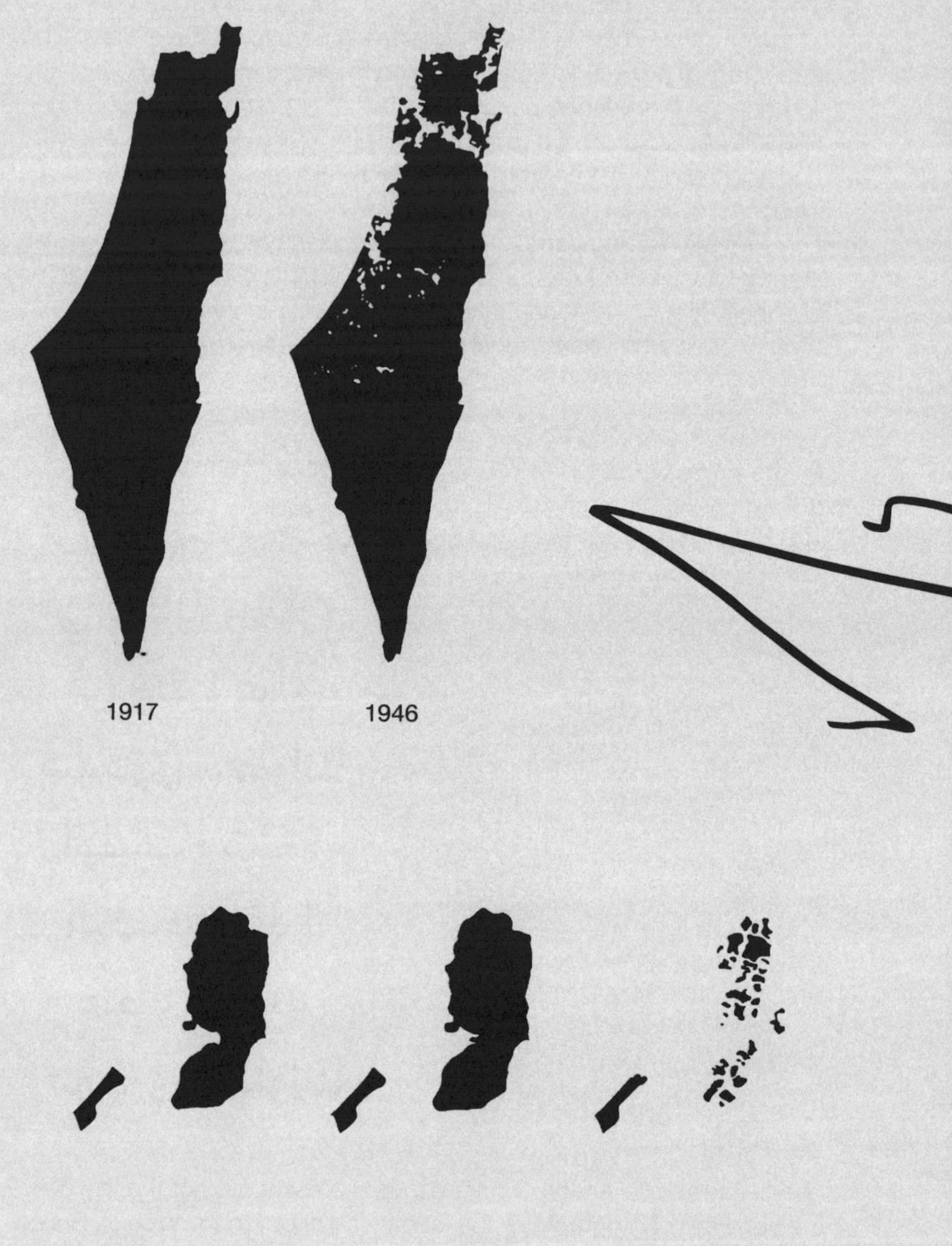
1917
1946
1948
1967
1967 - **

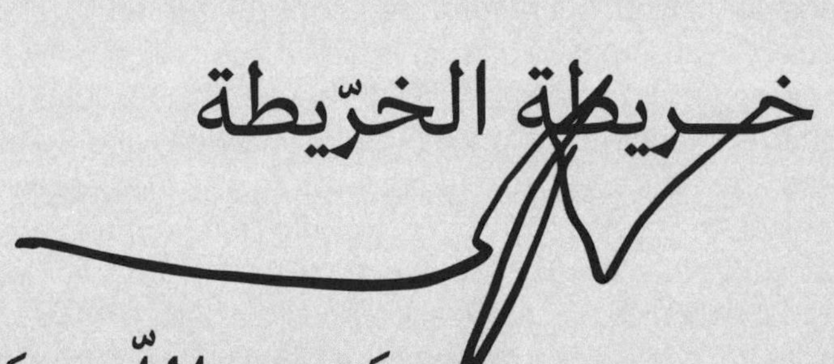

خريطة الخرّيطة

خَبّت اللّي خَبّط

ذكيّة وعَبيطة

سَلْبَت وْصَلْبت

ضيق النفس

هون صار عادات وتقاليد

وما فش حدا مواطن

An image not of land, but of ***territory,***[6] shrinking, tightening, asphyxiating. It is a convenient summary of loss, flattened into cartography, the colonial idiom of claims and treaties. Palestine's foundational presence is reduced to an underhanded memorandum between one Sykes and one Picot and a smattering of coastal settlements. It is the beginning of our containment, the conversion of our land into "territory" and our people into "populations." "Things were good then," this map preemptively assures us, "when the land was still called Palestine." But by exalting nomenclature, however sentimental, we bypass Britain's bloody occupation and role in abetting Jewish colonial settlement. We also overlook the fact that the West carved our lands into a synthetic bordered region labeled "the Middle East" (of Europe, that is). Before 1948, we are told, Palestine was peaceful, devoid of the feudalists who conspired with colonists and accelerated the expropriation of the worker's plot. It is a Palestine of abundance, of boundless, miraculously fertile orange groves, disassociated from the exploitation of the indigenous working class.

ظَلَمِت يلّلي حَكَمِت عالأَبطـــال بالإعدام

فؤاد والزير والـــــجمجوم راحوا غْـــــدام

واللّهِ من حين مـــا قرِّ الــــقرار بِعْدام

وانا مْـــــقَرَّحِ الجِفِن من كثر البكـا ونـواح[7]

This idyllic precursor, emptied of revolutionary struggle, lulls us into a false sense of security, setting the stage for the high drama of 1948: the expulsion of over half of the Palestinian population by Zionist militias. The once solid expanse of land is now fractured, its

6
Samera Esmeir makes an important distinction between land and territory, noting that the latter is a colonial juridical category: "Israel's obliterative machinery is no longer satisfied with targeting the Palestinian inhabitation of the land, which the same machinery juridically classified as Israeli territory decades ago [emphasis added]." Samera Esmeir, "The End of Colonial Government," in *From the River to the Sea: Essays for a Free Palestine*, eds. Sai Englert, Michal Schatz, and Rosie Warren (London: Verso, 2023).

7
قصيدة للفرّان فهد الجلبوش كتبت في أعقاب إعدام المقاومين الشهداء محمد خليل أبو جمجوم وعطا الزير وفؤاد حجازي. انظر إياد معلوف، ««مِنْ سجن عكّا»: كيف تفاعلت صحف فلسطين مع إعدام المناضلين الثلاثة؟»عرب ٤٨، ٢٠٢١، https://www.arab48.com/فسحة/ورق/آخر/2021/09/08/-من-سجن-عكا--كيف-تفاعلت-صحف-فلسطين-مع-إعدام-المناضلين-الثلاثة.

people driven into militarily bound territories. Palestinian presence is cartographically excised as hollowed out zones in the negative—a landlocked patch to the east and a coastal sliver to the southwest, administered respectively by the British-installed monarchies of Jordan (the east bank) and Egypt. Pushed to the margins, we are cordoned and contained by the so-called green line, whose ink has since run, bleeding into the edges of an ever-tightening territory.

Villages, cities, and entire districts are eradicated to make way for settler infrastructure, resulting in topographic devastation and historical erasure. Integral to this process is the systematic replacement of indigenous place names with foreign biblical Hebraic ones, a colonial mission initiated by Protestant Europeans in the mid-nineteenth century that Zionist settler-colonists later adopted.[8] This renaming campaign is more than cosmetic change; it is an ideological transformation that interpellates the land as innately Jewish and "restored" from its "false Oriental heirs." In its compulsion to erase, settler-colonialism may reinscribe indigenous place names—not as sites of history or tradition, but as markers of massacre and death. What do we know of Tantura, Deir Yassin, Qibya, Kufr Qassim, and Sabra and Shatila beyond the massacres they endured? And Rafah, Khan Yunis, Beit Lahia, and Jabalia prompt the harrowing question: ***which massacre?*** What seems like a contradiction actually reveals the brutal logic of colonialism: recurrent massacres harden these places into zones of normalized killing, producing them as nonplaces. They eradicate their distinctness, their customs, that subtle lilt in their accent that carries thousands of years of history. Each new atrocity not only adds to the tally of violence but also erases the memory of previous massacres, creating a cycle of uncommemorable death. As a result, our geography is learned and our sense of place established through a history of destruction and negation. Palestinian deaths, and not lives, are inscribed in these nonplaces, as an absented presence in the negative. But how can the planar language of geography capture the emotional weight of massacre? And where in that linear image of Catastrophe are we to locate repeated episodes of slaughter?

8
The colonial project of mapping and renaming Palestine was formalized by the British-run Palestine Exploration Fund (PEF) in 1865. This imperial endeavor encompassed not only the renaming of the land but also a historical rewriting and appropriation through archaeological excavations. For more information on the PEF, see their peer-reviewed journal, *The Palestine Exploration Quarterly*, founded in 1865. For further reading on the Zionist continuation and expansion of this British imperial endeavor, see Nadia Abu el-Haj's *Facts on the Ground: Archaeological Practice and Territorial Self-Fashioning in Israeli Society* (Chicago: University of Chicago Press, 2001).

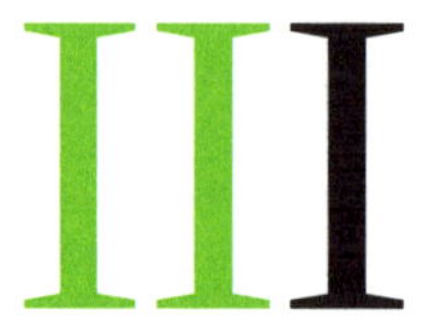

Being where you are,
being where you are
not allowed to be
..
We find ourselves in the lack.[9]

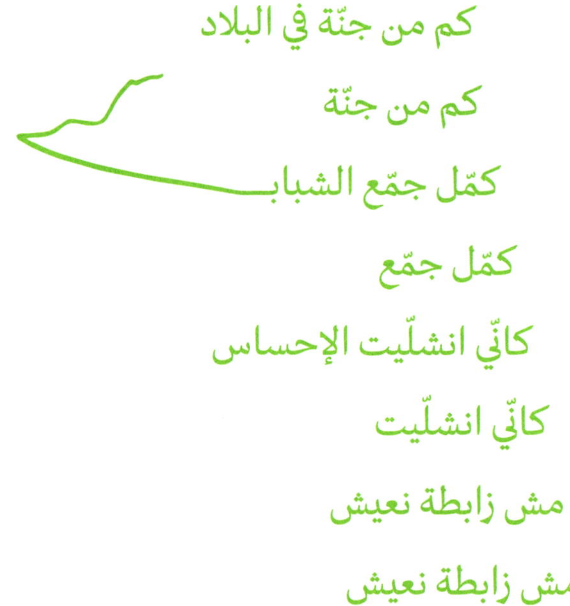

From the colonist's perspective, the native always appears in the negative, surfacing as an avowed repression. Nasser Abou-Rahme theorized this as "settler negation," explaining it as follows: "To negate is neither simply to destroy something nor, as the dictionary definition would have it, to 'deny the existence' of something. Negation is related to, but distinct from both destruction and denial, as well as foreclosure and repudiation. To negate ***is to refute the presence of something you also and simultaneously accept exists***."[10]

أَيا مكانا، هَيْنا فكلامَك
واقف مع إنّي مِش موجود
صافن في ابني المِش مولود
تحت قصف الكذبة

9
Abbas and R. Abou-Rahme, *May amnesia*, 2021-.

10
Nasser Abourahme, "Beneath the Concrete: Camp, Colony, Palestine," PhD diss., (Columbia University, 2019), 226–7.

In affirming the native's nonexistence, settler negation inherently concedes to an existence of the native, however liminal. The very grammar of negation demands some relationship to the repressed subject: its utterance, even if in the negative. In Arabic, the negative is grammatically divided into two categories: negation or ***al-nafī*** (النفي) and prohibition or ***al-nahī*** (النهي). While negation (***al-nafī***) spans all tenses, perpetuating an all-encompassing ontological absence ("There was/is/will be no such thing as Palestine/Palestinians"), prohibition *(**al-nahī**)* only exists in the present tense, issuing commands against an immediate or ongoing action ("Do not refer to it as Palestine;" "Do not live as a Palestinian;" Or simply, "***do not exist.***") The interplay of negation and prohibition reveals a deeper contradiction: Palestinians are simultaneously declared nonexistent and yet prohibited from existing. But how can one forbid what supposedly does not exist?

بِعْ عينُه　　　　هاد مِش أنا

مِش أرض هاي　　　　أكيد هاي مِش سما

The terms *nafī* and *nahī* also offer us a framework from which to understand the ontological negation of Palestinians and the continued prohibition on our being. *Nafī*, from the root n/f/y (ن/ف/ي) has two primary and connected meanings: 1. Negation, denial, refusal, and disavowal, and 2. Banishment and exile. The catastrophic expulsion of Palestinians is read as a negation of self; the banishment from the land is the banishment of the self. Derived from the same root, the word *al-manfiyyūn* [المنفيّون] does not merely refer to the exiled but to those who are ontologically negated and disavowed. The exiled are thus recipients of a double violence—physical banishment and existential negation. Similarly, *al-manfā* [المنفى] refers not only to exile but also to the negative space—anywhere but Palestine—in which exiles are forced to live in the negative.

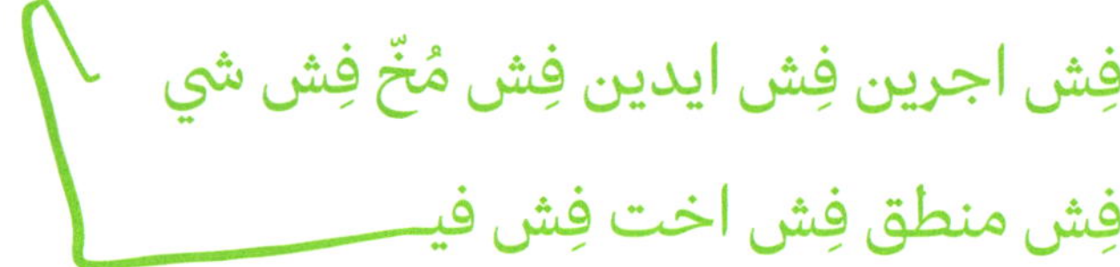

أنا مَسْكة اللّحن، أنا السّالب. أنا فَلْتة عاللّحن، أنا السّالب.

السّالب بشلّك، هيك بتحكي الأسطورة

السّالب بشلّك، هيك بتحكي العصفورة

Nahī, from the root n/h/y (ن/ه/ي), means prohibition, forbiddance, or setting a limit on something, typically in an ethical or moral context. This is embodied in the prohibitive particle “lā/لا” (“do not”), used to issue commands or injunctions to prohibit an action. Derived from the same root, the causative form *anhā* (أنهى) means to finish, complete, or bring to an end. It indicates not just the act of setting a limit but ensuring that it is ultimately realized and enforced to its final consequence. Both prohibition and completion are based on defining and enforcing limits, whether it is an immediate constraint or a final endpoint. We can stretch this linguistic threshold further into a physical one: borders, checkpoints, walls, and sieges, which mark the limit of our existence. The negative prohibitive particle *lā*/*لا* is materially pronounced in the architecture of repression and prohibition, demarcating the limit of being and breathing. By articulating the limit of our existence, the physical barriers admit to our being; they follow the grammar of negation, which betrays the ontological denial of the native (our nonexistence) by conceding that there *is* a Palestinian existence to limit, prohibit, and end.

في شمال شرق داخل الخارج الغربي المشتّت
أنا أكتر، بس أنقص، من محبوس بِتْفَتْفَت
وما في أفخر منّي حاليًّا عاللّي نبَّت
اقطعوا نصّ الوقت من قِشْرُه
من خِشْنُه
مش فارقة. حتّى لو فَرْقَت

11
Abbas and Abou-Rahme, 2021.

To view Palestine in the negative is to witness the protracted violence of repression and erasure, to see our own death image slowly processing before us. In this image of Catastrophe, colonial violence is evidenced by absence; it lies in the lack, in the negation of the land and its people.[11] Our continued existence is juridically recoded as "present absentees," "refugees," "stateless persons," "infiltrators," "terrorists," "temporary residents." In short, a nonpeople. We, in the lack, do not inhabit a land but ***an orientation*** (the west bank is a direction relative to an imperially conjectured kingdom); ***a strip*** (the district of Gaza is shrunk, severed, and sequestered into a coastal crevice); ***a half*** (Jerusalem is sliced into two); ***a time*** (the remainder of Palestine is referred to in the suspended time of Catastrophe: 1948); and ***an exterior*** (the disavowed exiles, beginning with the refugee camps scattered across Syria, Lebanon, and Jordan, and extending to rest of the world). The sixth geography, as the Palestinian scholar Abdul-Rahim al-Shaikh pointed out, is the Zionist prison.[12]

12
Abdul-Rahim al-Shaikh, "Al-Makān al-Muwāzī: Rasm al-Zaman fī Fikr Walīd Daqqa" [The Parallel Place: Drawing Time in the Thought of Walid Daqqa], *Journal for Palestine Studies*, no. 135 (2023): 204–5. See also al-Shaikh's seminar series with imprisoned leaders of the Palestinian national movement Marwan Barghouti, Walid Daqqa, Abdul-Razzeq Farraj, Abdul-Nasser Issa, Wajdi Joudeh, Basim Khandaqji, and Thabet Mardawi, "Nadwat al-Ḥaraka al-Filasṭīniyya al-Asīra: al-Jughrāfiyā al-Sādisa [Seminar on the Palestinian Prisoners' Movement: The Sixth Geography], *Journal for Palestine Studies*, no. 128 (2021): 9–59.

بتعمل اشي، بعاقبوا الكلّ
ليبطلوا كلّ
خطّة قديمة لَيْرَبّوا الضّوء
مِش لازم نجمّل الواقع
شَلَّحوا وشَوَّهوا العايش والمَيّت
فش غير في "دثّريني" جمال في اللّجوء
تشويه نفسي
وين ما كنّا
ما احنا وين ما كنا
ذنبنا بسوق
حتّى الأسرى بحسّوا بذَنْب
الزنزانة منفى
جوّاتها كمان منفى
وليد شَرَح انتصارُه
بفكّر في اللي حكاه وبَحاوِل أروق
الله يرحمه

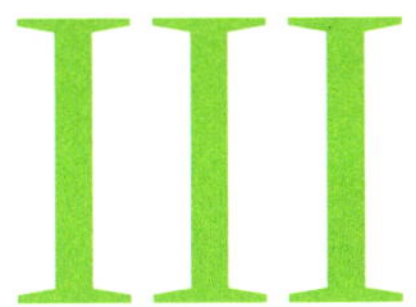

Writing from Gilboa prison in 2009, the Palestinian intellectual Walid Daqqa observed that the occupation prisons, the sixth geography, were microcosms of Palestine, mirroring the larger colonial fragmentation of the land.[13] Situated beyond the colonial wall and the Faqqūʿa Mountain range—where natural topography is exploited as a border—Gilboa prison is designated for Palestinians from the northern west bank, specifically Tulkarem, Nablus, and Jenin, with segregated sections for those from Jerusalem and 1948. Daqqa described Gilboa and other colonial penitentiaries as "micro-prisons" [سجون صغيرة] nested within the macro-prison of colonized Palestine [السجن الكبير]. In the micro-prison, as in Palestine, Palestinians continue to be forcibly separated from one another in segregated wings and cells mirroring the land's fragmentation. While the term apartheid is widely used to describe the Palestinian case, Daqqa noted its inadequacy in capturing the colonial segregation of Palestinians.[14] By centering the racial divide between "Jews" and "Arabs,"[15] the framing of apartheid overlooks and even eclipses the Zionist-engineered segregation of Palestinians from one another. Daqqa's argument therefore hinges on a territorial rather than a racial divide, emphasizing the colonial reconstitution

13
Walid Nimr Daqqa, *Ṣahr al-Waʿī, aw fi Iʿādat Taʿrīf al-Taʿdhīb* [Melting of Consciousness, or On Redefining Torture] (Beirut: Arab Scientific Publishers, 2010).

14
Daqqa, *Ṣahr al-Waʿī*, 32.

15
The very categorical division of "Jew" and "Arab," which disavows the existence of Jewish Arabs, was colonially constructed before any infrastructural apartheid existed. Moreover, as Mahmood Mamdani reminds us, apartheid was presented as a solution—diplomatically repackaged into the "two-state solution"—rather than a problem. Mahmood Mamdani, "Edward W. Said and the Question of Palestine," Faculty Panel, Columbia University, New York, April 26, 2024.

of Palestine as prison. Within the sixth geography, imprisoned Palestinians continue to be reshuffled and segregated from one another through what Daqqa described as "deportations" [ترحيلات] and "transfers" [تنقيلات],[16] echoing foundational Zionist strategies of Palestinian expulsion and displacement.[17] This creates a perpetual state of separation and estrangement, mirroring the fragmentation of Palestine itself—from a collective to a fractured body, from a people to isolated individuals. His description highlights the cycle of banishment within the prison system, begging the question: from the sixth geography, where else is there to go?

حاسس حالي فكيس نايلون
بِدَربونا نعيش بفُقاعات أمنية زي كيث دايتون[18]

مُختَبَرْ ومَصْنَعْ
بالمُخْتَصَرْ لِمْقَطَّعْ

جوا المخ عِدّ كَمْ بركان
مْخَبّيهُم عن عين سجّان
ماسك حالي فألف حزام

مِتْعَوِّد عالحَشْرَة من الاجتياح

ضَرَبات لحِّق، هذا جزء من الجزء

Administering entire populations as prisoners involves more than confinement; it exerts deep psychological control. Daqqa's central thesis is that this layered carceral geography functions as a tool to reshape Palestinian consciousness [إعادة صهر الوعي الفلسطيني]. The "micro-prisons," in particular, target resistant Palestinians, aiming not just to detain and isolate those deemed a "security threat" but to weaken their resolve. It is a cognitive rewiring that seeks to fundamentally quash any resistance and reprogram how Palestinians view their struggle, beginning with the most steadfast and principled.[19] Zionism's bid to melt and remold Palestinian consciousness is premised on severing our ontological bond with the land. By physically segregating us from one another, it imposes a restricted sense of belonging, not to the land and its people but to an enclosed territory and population. Palestinians are subsequently reclassified from the physically and spiritually rooted "people of the land" [أصحاب الأرض], to the legally tenuous "present absentees" [الحاضرون الغائبون] and "residents of the occupied territories" [سكّان الأراضي المحتلّة]. This physical and categorical splitting from the land is an existential negation, which, as Samera Esmeir expressed, "[turns] Palestinians into empty vessels, evacuating their souls."[20] Once the relationship to the land is cut, so too is our peoplehood. By this, we do not mean a lament of a lost arcadia, but a material and ontological constitution that extends to time, now disjointed from its natural course. Instead of living with the ecological rhythm of the land, where time is plotted against seasons and harvests, Palestinian life is dictated by the oppressive episodes of colonial time. In this temporal framework, natural cycles become quarterly measures of productivity, harvests correspond to profit rather than sustenance, and indigenous life is reduced to its exchange value. While the Zionist apparatus is crafted to enforce our ontological negation, Palestinians continue to resist through armed struggle, popular uprisings, and everyday practices rooted in the land.

16
These terms appear several times in *Ṣahr al-Waʿī*, See, for instance, pages 61, 75, and 76.

17
For more on the Zionist idea and practice of transfer, see Nur Masalha's *Expulsion of the Palestinians: The Concept of "Transfer" in Zionist Political Thought, 1882-1948* (Washington, D.C.: Institute for Palestine Studies, 1992).

18
مقاطعة، آخر كلمة،
حيوان ناطق، ٢٠١٣.

19
Daqqa, *Ṣahr al-Waʿī*, 30.

20
Esmeir, 64.

غُلّ مِيْت سِنِة
الغضب هذا إلي
هُوْن هو رِبِي
صيف وشِتِي
انْبَسَط وشِقِي
انْهَدّ لَحَدّ ما هِدِي
الضِّفّة محَوّطة مِن جُوّا
جُندي فبُرْج، مِثل جِدِي

The conversion of land to territory to prison is most explicitly manifest in colonial labor operations. Feudalism, serfdom, slavery, apprenticeship, peonage, and other forms of forced and indentured labor centered around the lucrative cultivation of land emerge as disciplinary moral remedies compatible with colonial capital. The colonized/imprisoned/enslaved are accordingly diagnosed with a chronic moral malady, to be regulated through the "corrective" regimen of labor. They are quarantined in enclosed agricultural spaces (macro-prisons), which operate as surveillance technologies[21]—the plantation, the estate, the fief, and in Palestine, the *bayyāra*—intended to produce industrious subjects compliant with the demands of the colony and its metropolitan centers.

شو هالعَملة؟
شو العَمَل؟
أَبْرَد
أَغْرَب
أَعْقَد
شو هالعُملة؟
أَبْعَد
بَتْذَكّر كِتْفَك

As Zionism depends on expropriating Palestinian agricultural land for colonial settlement, Palestinian labor has shifted to industrial sectors, primarily construction.[22] The colonial stranglehold on industry, mobility, and trade has stifled and de-developed the Palestinian economy,[23] leading to high unemployment rates and a surplus labor force. As a result, working-class Palestinian men have become economically hostage to their colonizers, who control their access to employment through a paid permit system that mandates biometric data collection and cellular tracking.[24] In cruel colonial fashion, Palestinians find themselves building settlements on the very lands from which they were expelled.

كيف زعلان وانت اللي تركها؟ بالنّبي ياه...
كيف زعلان عالجدار واحنا اللي بنيناه؟
سامِع الشَّر؟

في ناس ماسكة البلد أمنيًّا
حاطة ناس ماسكة البلد أمنيًّا

ضفّة البنوك والشركات
خُد يا حرامي يا سراق

21
Krista Thompson, "The Evidence of Things Not Photographed: Slavery and Historical Memory in the British West Indies," *Representations* 113, no. 1 (2011): 39–71.

22
For a historical trajectory on the expropriation of Palestinian land for Zionist settlement, see Charles Anderson, "The British Mandate and the Crisis of Palestinian Landlessness, 1929–1936", *Middle Eastern Studies*, 54, no. 2 (2018), 171–215. On Palestinian labor under Zionism, see Andreas Hackl's "Occupied Labour: Dispossession Through Incorporation Among Palestinian Workers in Israel," *Settler Colonial Studies* 13, no. 1 (2023): 96–114.

23
Sara Roy, *The Gaza Strip: The Political Economy of De-development* (Washington, DC: Institute for Palestine Studies), 2016.

24
Meanwhile, the Zionist apparatus, in collaboration with the Palestinian authority, has engineered a privileged business elite through the issuance of a special permit known as the "Businessman Card" (BMC). This permit allows select Palestinians to traverse colonized land with relative freedom. Issued by colonial authorities following stringent "security" evaluations, the BMC system epitomizes economic stratification under colonialism. It grants elite entrepreneurs, predominantly from the west bank enhanced mobility and access across historic Palestine for commercial purposes. The BMC class represents a cross-colonial collusion, establishing a mutually advantageous arrangement for both colonizer and the comprador. Driven by profit and compliance, these elites perceive their fellow Palestinians not as a community but as consumers under an unshakeable colonial power.

Such a perverse system of exploitation is subsumed under the broader operations of settler-colonialism, which fluctuate between the management of life (biopolitics) and the management of death (necropolitics). Framed as a struggle to maintain a Jewish majority, Zionism's "demographic problem" is the Palestinians. Our existence is a persistent, reproductive obstacle that must be managed and ideally eliminated. Indigenous worth is depleted and gutted out, representing, as Frantz Fanon wrote, "not only the absence of values, but also the negation of values."[25] Whatever value retained is not inherent but economic, reducing Palestinians to units of production and consumption dictated by the market rate. Palestinian labor is negated and classified as unskilled, yet its extracted "negative value" yields surplus for the colonial regime, which further outsources our own division. Until Zionist necropower is perfected and Palestinians are completely eliminated, a profitable biopolitical program is implemented, managing us not as people, but as alienated consumers and surveilled stocks of labor. Zionism's "demographic crisis" is therefore converted into a profitable enterprise.

قَدَّم. استنّى. خُد. أخَد. انبَسَط.

صِحي. راكض. وقَّف. استنّى.

رِكِب. نِزِل. رِكِب. نِزِل. صَفّ.

استَنّى. استَنّى. فوت. فات.

يالله. شافْ. رَدّ. حَسّ. مَحى.

خَلَّص. خُد. أَخَد. اطلَع. طِلِع.

ارْجَع. تِرجَعِش. ارْجَع. اتّاخَدْ.

استَنّى. شاف. طِلِع. حَسّ.

This is but one ontological negation of Palestinians, their conversion into a soulless industrial army whose labor is severed from the land. Marx's theory of alienation is compounded under settler-colonial labor operations, as Palestinians are not only alienated from their labor—whose means and product they cannot own—but are compelled to produce the mechanisms of their alienation from the land.[26] Instead of engaging in self-actualizing labor, which fulfills the people's needs and provides home and hearth, Palestinians are forced to satisfy their colonists' gluttony at their own expense. It is not a labor of affirmation, but of denial,[27] so alienating that its very performance dislocates Palestinians from the land and disavows our being. This Catastrophe-d consciousness remains lodged in the Palestinian body, which, as Daqqa maintained, Zionism strives to melt and mold anew, hollowing out the memory of the Nakba and turning us into the "empty vessels" Esmeir speaks of. The memory of the Nakba is therefore both psychic and somatic, revived with every act of tearing down our homes and building the colonist's. Each white brick laid, red roof tile pitched, and stone façade installed reiterates the story of Palestinian dispossession, locking it in as muscle memory.

تشويه عن طريق التدمير   تشويه عن طريق البنى
بس لسا مقروء.
هدّوا بيته وبيت عَزاه   وأخطر اشي ينسمحلنا فيه
هو الهدوء.

25
Frantz Fanon, *The Wretched of the Earth*, trans. Constance Farrington (New York, Grove Press, 1963), 41.

26
Karl Marx, "Estranged Labour," in *Economic and Philosophic Manuscripts of 1844*, trans. Martin Milligan (New York: Dover Publications, 2007), 67–83. See also Adam HajYahia, "The Principle of Return: The Repressed Ruptures of Zionist Time," *Parapraxis* (2024), https://www.parapraxismagazine.com/articles/the-principle-of-return.

27
Marx, 72.

"Only in Jerusalem does the stone that was extracted and quarried from the mountain rocks appear alien to the mountains themselves,"[28] remarked Palestinian intellectual Azmi Bishara. Even in its appropriation of local materials, settler architecture remains artificial and empty. Indeed, much of the appropriated limestone is a veneer masking the cheap, mass-produced settler structures. This surface-level cladding is replicated in settlements across the west bank in an attempt to forge continuity with the perennially expanding borders of Jerusalem.[29] Like the alienated Palestinians whose land and labor are external to themselves, the Jerusalem stone itself is alienated, as it remains external to the building's structural function.

"بِدنا ايّاه زيّه، بس مش زيّه بالزّبط
حامِض حِلو
شوي من هون، شوي من هون
لمسة فَلحة ورَشّة بِدو
فِش داعي للقلق
ولا حدا يروح يِتْلَصَّص
بنجيبهم هُمّ يسّووا
وشوف كيف الهَوا بِتْقَصقَص
مش بس بِدنا ايّاهم ينسوا
بِدنا الذِّكرى يطير معناها
انجنّ الرّوبوت قال في روح
صلحوه، ولو رَفَض، كِبّوا العاهة"
بِعّ عينُه

On the one hand, Zionists appropriated Palestinian vernacular architecture, claiming it as their own; on the other, they viewed it with disdain, defining their buildings in stark opposition to ours.[30] These projections are not contradictory, but rather stem from an ambivalent colonial consciousness that renders indigenous architecture both beautiful and primitive, or beautiful ***because*** it is primitive.[31] Grounded in a "rational" European modernist ethos, the early settlements were designed in direct contrast to our "irrational"[32] village homes, exemplifying Theodor Herzl's colonial vision of an "outpost of civilisation as opposed to barbarism."[33]

28
Azmi Bishara, *Al-Ḥājiz: Shaẓāyā Riwāya* [The Checkpoint: Fragments of a Narrative] (Beirut: Arab Cultural Center, 2006), 16. See also Eyal Weizman, *Hollow Land: Israel's Architecture of Occupation* (London: Verso, 2007), 33.

29
Even Zionism's manufactured indigeneity is itself unoriginal, inheriting the practice of preserving and promoting Jerusalem stone exteriors from a 1918 British ordinance. See British military governor Ronald Storr's preface in Pro-Jerusalem Society Council, *Jerusalem, 1918–1920*, ed. Charles Robert Ashbee (London: John Murray, 1921). See also Annabel Wharton, "Jerusalem Remade," in *Modernism and the Middle East: Architecture and Politics in the Twentieth Century*, eds. Sandy Isenstadt and Kishwar Rizvi (Seattle: University of Washington Press, 2008), 39-60, and Nadi Abusaada, "Urban Encounters: Imaging the City in Mandate Palestine," in *Imaging and Imagining Palestine: Photography, Modernity and the Biblical Lens, 1918–1948*, eds. Karène Sanchez Summerer and Sary Zananiri (Leiden: Brill, 2021), 370–371.

30
In a 1908 address to the Jewish Colonization Society of Vienna, Arthur Ruppin, the German "father of Zionist settlement," declared that "in contrast to the pitiful Arab villages with their huts of baked clay, the Jewish colonies, with their wide streets, their strong stone houses, and their red-tiled roofs look like veritable oases of culture." Arthur Ruppin, *Three Decades of Palestine* (Jerusalem: Schocken, 1936), 9; Wharton, "Jerusalem Remade," 45.

31
As Thomas Leitersdorf, the architect of the Ma'ale Adumim settlement (on the Palestinian lands of Ezariyya and Abu Dis), admitted, "I look upon the morphology of the Arab villages with envy. The beauty of the Arab village lies in its accumulative and somewhat irrational nature." Eran Tamir-Tawil, "To start a city from scratch: an interview with architect Thomas m. Leitersdorf," in *A civilian occupation: The Politics of Israeli Architecture*, eds. Rafi Segal and Eyal Weizman (Tel Aviv and London: Babel and Verso Press, 2003), 160; cited in Weizman, *Hollow Land*, 44.

32
Weizman, 44.

33
Theodor Herzl, *A Jewish State: An Attempt at a Modern Solution of the Jewish Question*, trans. Sylvie D'Avigdor (New York: The Maccabaean Publishing Company, 1904), 29. The gated (walled) Garden City style modernism of Zionist settlements further invoke a sense of familiarity for European populations transplanted to a foreign land. (This is not unlike the flammable forests of invasive pine species planted by the Jewish National Fund (JNF) atop razed Palestinian villages both to conceal our trace and fabricate continuity with European landscapes). For more on the JNF's ecologically hazardous forest enterprise, see Areej Ashhab and Marta Wódz, "Between The Pines: More-than-human Narratives beyond the Jewish National Fund Forests," in *Researching Palestine*, eds. Ala Abed, Chris Harding, and Maria Khoury (Dar Jacir, 2024): 47–55.

Forcefully grafting himself onto the land, the colonizer remains conspicuously foreign. His imported environments exhibit not a natural ecological cohesion but, as Edward Said put it, "a rude interventionary power," spreading and consuming our lands like a "marching cancer."[34]

مستعمرة جمبُه لبيتي مبسوطة
عحالها من بعيد بتغاوز

بتضلها تكبر سرطان عالجبل
نفسها تنزل تطردنا أنا عارف

The colonial effort to suppress the fact of dispossession aims to deter the inevitability of return, for without any recollection of the land, we have neither an entity to resist nor an object to recover. The refusal of Palestinians to concede to the finality of their loss and accept the death (and therefore irrecoverability) of Palestine, is, as Joseph Massad argues, colonially diagnosed as an affliction.[35] Zionism has specifically pathologized the Palestinian people's attachment to the land—our unwillingness to forget or forgo its loss—as a psychological disorder it calls antisemitism,[36] which can only be remedied through a resection of the "diseased" Palestinian mind (melting of consciousness) or the culling of the resistant masses (total extermination). Zionism's exploitative labor structure is one widely administered remedy for the homesickness of Palestinians. By erasing the trace and foreclosing the possibility of a homeland, the colonist asserts that there is no home—***and never was***—to be homesick over. The recursive act of building the colony reinforces the loss of home by literally cementing settler presence and reproducing our own alienation. Palestinians are compelled to build their own cage, brick by brick, wall by wall in a tormenting cycle that converts the land into a prison. The mortifying routine of waking up at four in the morning and trudging from ford to ford,[37] from checkpoint to checkpoint, factoring in the hours of degradation—where an hour-long commute can take anywhere from three to nine hours depending on the colonist's mood—in order to make it to work on time epitomizes this estrangement. It is a labor that negates land and self, repeatedly displacing us from every "here" we inhabit to produce us as strangers who have "never been"—never been present, never been expelled or dispossessed, never been here and one with the land.

كيلوَك ٣ دقايق
كيلُوي ٣ ساعات

34
Edward Said, *After the Last Sky, Palestinian Lives* (New York: Pantheon Books, 1986), 72.

35
Massad, "The Cultural Work of Recovering Palestine," 2015.

36
Massad, 188: "The Palestinians, while grieving the loss of their dead and their way of life, their expulsion from their homes and lands, and their loss of independence to Israeli control, still resist mourning the loss of Palestine since 1948 as a final loss, continuing instead to invoke their attachment to it and affirm and plan for its recovery. This insistence has been judged by the enemies of the Palestinians as pathological and is often identified as 'anti-Semitic,' itself a psychoanalytically diagnosed pathology. In a psychoanalytic sense, the Zionist charge amounts to characterizing (an alleged) Palestinian anti-Semitism as a reaction-formation to an imputed Palestinian failure to mourn."

37
Fords are seven-seater vans used for public transport in the west bank, with the name generically applied to all such vans regardless of their actual manufacturer.

IV

كان برتاح لونهم أشباح
ما بخّوفنيش صدى الرياح
ما بتخوّفنيش العتمة بتاتًا
انا لمخّوفني معيش سلاح

المعظم عدوّ

38
In reading colonial histories comparatively, Massad has pointed out that "the question of proximate partying is hardly unique to Israelis. A South African attorney-general in the then South African-occupied settler colony of Namibia stated in 1983 that the white 'public haven't the foggiest idea what's going on in the operational area,' where black resistance was active. 'Whites in the south,' he said, 'continue to have parties.'" Massad, "Israel-Palestine war: How Israel and the West Smear the Palestinians as Antisemitic," *Middle East Eye*, November 15, 2023, https://www.middleeasteye.net/opinion/israel-west-smear-palestinians-antisemitic.

39
بيت من قصيدة «يا ظلام السجن خيّم» للصحفي السوري المناضل نجيب الريّس، التي «وردت على لسان الشهيد محمد خليل أبو جمجوم عندما أبلغه مدير سجن عكا البريطاني هو ورفيقاه عطا الزير وفؤاد حجازي بقرار الإعدام فشرعوا في ترديد النشيد يا ظلام السجن خيم وتم تنفيذ حكم الإعدام فيهم صباح الثلاثاء 17/6/1930.» أسامة الأشقر، "«يا ظلام السجن خيّم» حكاية مع نشيد خالد!" الجزيرة، ٢٠١٧، https://www.aljazeera.net/blogs/2017/10/18/يا-ظلام-السجن-خيم-حكاية-مع-نشيد-خالد.

40
See Patrick Wolfe's *Settler Colonialism and the Transformation of Anthropology: The Politics and Poetics of an Ethnographic Event* (New York: Continuum, 1998); and "Settler Colonialism and the Elimination of the Native," *Journal of Genocide Research* 8, no. 4 (2006): 387–409. See also Lorenzo Veracini, "Defending Settler Colonial Studies," *Australian Historical Studies* 45, no. 3 (2014): 311–16. For the theorization of the ongoing Nakba, see the late Elias Khoury's *Al-Nakba al-Mustamirra* (Beirut: Dār al-Ādāb, 2023).

Zionism's negation of the Palestinian subject, that "we are not" and "have never been," is not just a repression of our presence or a denial of our peoplehood; rather, these actions are screens for the true repressed content: the looming threat of Palestinian return. The image of return is so deeply repressed in the Zionist psyche that a trance music festival for "peace" can be held next to a population kept under siege for over seventeen years without any perceived contradiction.[38] Settlers can afford these delusions and remain in a state of colonial hypnosis precisely because they cage and bury the native. Neither the siege of Gaza nor the suffering it has engendered are repressed by settler psyches; on the contrary, they are starkly visible and actively enforced by Zionist policies and public opinion. Indeed, the death and abjection caused by the siege are not hidden but exhaustively reported on, counted, and evidenced. How many more politicians need to describe Gaza as an "open-air prison"? How much more evidence must be accrued, and how many more trials need to be adjourned? Who are all these human rights reports drafted for? And what other statistics could possibly be left to count? This cacophonous litany only conceals the imperative and inevitability of return, which remains bolted and shut under layers of colonial and neoliberal governance.

لا حامي حالي ولا الحَوَلَي في هاي اللحظة، عم بَمُرّ بموقف
أصعب من كلشي شفته، الصراحة بدي مساعدة
كل جانب من عيشتي ضاوي طوارئ عندي في زعل هين
يا دوب أنا عايش بس راضي هسّا و باللي جاي بعدين
لسّا بنحكي عن صاحب الأرض هندي، بالله عليك

يا ظلامَ القبرِ خيّمْ إنّنا نهوى الظلاما
ليسَ بعدَ الموتِ إلّا فجرُ مجدٍ يتسامى[39]

While the Nakba embodies the important theoretical assertion that colonialism is a structure rather than an isolated event,[40] there lies a danger in reifying it. Structure can imply permanence, stasis, routine, even irreversibility. The Nakba is structurally ongoing, but the Catastrophic state it spawns is neither permanent nor absolute. The colonist's impulse to archive the Nakba reflects his desire to look past the Catastrophe, to move beyond it by suspending Palestinians in the ***already passed*** tense, where Zionism must rebury our saturated image of return. Atop the rubble, the colonist manufactures his illusion of progress, the brittle and hollow stone façade feigning continuity, screening the repressed Palestinian village whose ruins patiently await reactivation.[41] The colonist does not produce history (for he has no rooted past to build upon) but represses it. His narrative is one of distortions, deluding himself into belonging while concealing his fear of indigenous return.

نعامة ترفصك
بيلبس ثوب فلسطيني وبِدْبِك يعني بِرُقْصَك.[42]

كم واحد منهم غيّر اسمه لمّا دخل
حواكير، شوارع فيها أصوات تاريخ ودم
بتعرف إنه السلام أجدد وإنّه الحرب أقدم؟

In contrast, it is the resistant masses who oil the machinery of history. The repression of Palestinians in Zionist psyches arises from both the incompletion of the Nakba and the persistence of Palestinian resistance. As Palestinian thinker Khaled Odetallah reminds us, "The Nakba, in its ground operations, was not purely a catastrophe; it also encompassed resistance and fighting until the last bullet," which continues to this day.[43] When we speak of an ongoing Nakba, we address both the Catastrophe-d Palestinian condition and the continuous effort to resist it. Driven by the conviction to return, resistance deepens our relationship to the land, affirming our existence not as soulless vessels of melted consciousness but as a people yearning for liberation.

قَدْ ما طاخ الطيخ ما بهمّش
بدوّخ رصاصة
فِش تصيبيني يا مَكّارة
وين أنا، ما بتعرفيش أي حارة
بلّشتي تْخَبْصي واتدعسي عاللّاصة

41
Abbas and R. Abou-Rahme, *And yet my mask is powerful*, 2016.

42
مقاطعة، ٢٠١٣.

43
Khaled Odetallah, "Khaled Odetallah: Filasṭīn min al-Quds ilā Gaza," Interview by Abdul-Rahim al-Shaikh, *Al-Nakba al-Mustamirra*, no. 137 (2024): 70.

Palestinian intellectual and martyr Basil al-Araj,[44] whom Odetallah continues to honor in his writing, described resistance as an act of enduring value and significance [المقاومة جدوى مستمرة] whose social and historical benefits continue to appreciate. "Every price you pay in resistance, if not reaped in your lifetime, will be reaped in due course," wrote al-Araj.[45] To invest in resistance is to believe in the inevitability of an otherwise, where the line between life and afterlife, breath and martyrdom is not so thin. It is an investment that generates multiple returns: a return to the land, to the self and the collective, a return of innumerable social and cultural worth, and a return of the repressed. In a history tour around the Jenin district, al-Araj explained that Jenin's investment in resistance against British occupation and Zionist colonial settlement during the 1930s was compounded over seven decades later after its people brought an end to the four settlements surrounding their camp and district in 2005.[46] Gaza's decisive liberation that same year, which culminated in the dismantling of twenty one settlements and dozens of military posts, affirmed the imperative of resistance and demonstrated that the return on its investment is indeed a tangible restoration and return to the land.[47]

44
In Arabic, al-Araj is referred to as "المثقف المشتبك" which roughly translates to "the engaged intellectual," referring to his an embroiled commitment to political struggle. Al-Araj himself had stressed the importance of political engagement, famously declaring, "If you want to become an intellectual, you must become engaged; if you do not want to become engaged [...] then away with you and your intellect" [بدك تصير مثقف، بدك تصير مشتبك، ما بدك تشتبك..بلا منك وبلا من ثقافتك]. Basil al-Araj, *Ṣawṭī Wāḍiḥ* [My Voice is Clear] (Beirut: Dār al-Mawwada, 2022), 13.

45
Al-Araj, *Ṣawṭī Wāḍiḥ*, 74. Unlike NGO-sponsored "activism," which prioritizes short-term goals aligned with donor agendas and funding cycles, resistance is a sustained struggle whose ultimate aim is liberation. After Oslo, Palestinian activism was systematically institutionalized, leading to the dissolution of civil society and grassroots efforts that had historically formed the backbone of popular resistance. This shift resulted in individualized projects emphasizing immediate, measurable outcomes rather than the long-term goal of liberation. For more on the NGO-ization of Palestine, see Sari Hanafi and Linda Tabar, The Emergence of a Palestinian Globalized Elite: Donors, International Organizations, and Local NGOs (Michigan: University of Michigan, 2009).

46
Al-Araj, "المقاومة وجدواها..نموذج ريف جنين" [The Resistance and its Efficacy..The Model of Jenin's Rural Areas], December 19, 2014, دائرة سليمان الحلبي للدراسات الاستعمارية والتحرر المعرفي [The Sulaiman Al-Halabi Center for Colonial Studies and Epistemic Liberation], Youtube video, 2:04, https://www.youtube.com/watch?v=NIoiBnZep_0&list=PLB8AcJNYKTPAQW0eIGgqSfGhKZXIrsp2V.

47
Enforced as a form of collective punishment for Gaza's resistance, the colonial siege has barred the full realization of this investment. Nevertheless, Gaza continues to invest in resistance and liberation, as seen in the Marches of Return in 2011, which were prematurely aborted only to be resumed in 2018–19 and again in 2023. These are only select episodes in what is a continuous investment and commitment to return.

يا ********* ~~~~

يويا

جيناكم غفلة

يويا

من فوق وتحتا

يويا

سوّينا زحمة

يويا

قلنا بِع عينه

يويا

قلنا يا عيبه

يويا

لأوّل مرة

يويا

اتزَلّط أبو شقرة

يويا

ميّة وخمسين

يويا

عام في التّكوين

يويا

أعرجنا صادِق

يويا

كل خطوة فادت

اخ يرحم روحك

"On October 7, 2023," stated Odetallah, "the Nakba did not appear ongoing [as a structure] but rather as a sudden historical event when refugees from the villages of the Gaza district actually returned to their homes."[48] Rather than placing the Nakba under archival lock and key or theorizing it as a structure, resistance and return aim to bring Catastrophe to a close. The role of resistance is not to come up with political solutions, but to affirm and practice the imperative (and not right) of return.[49] Al-Aqsa Flood is the return of the repressed, bursting past the settler's physical and psychic screens that propped up decades of death and degradation. It represents a tear in Zionist time, pushing against the colonial hour, and a rupture of the Zionist plane, where the "parallel time" of the micro-prison meets the "social time" of the macro-prison.[50] The resistance's resolve to free Palestinian prisoners must be read as part of a larger imperative of return, where the six geographies converge.

قبل حدعشر سنة
صحّلّي أتعرّف عليه
كان لسّا طالع من حبسة حدعشر سنة
قال لي "في تاريخ الشعوب اللي قاومت،
٤٪ منهم بس اللي بقاوموا
احنا النسبة عِنّا كتير أعلى
فاتّطّمّن"
"سأقول ما لا تحتمله حضارة الآخرين.."[51]
..حياتنا أثمن من حياة المستعمِرين.

48
Odetallah and al-Shaikh (2024): 70.

49
Bishara, "فلسطين قضية العرب أم مشكلة الفلسطينيين؟ أسئلة النكبة و التاريخ" [Palestine: An Arab Cause or a Palestinian Problem? Questions of the Nakba and History], May 18, 2009, American University of Beirut, 1:47:31, Live streamed and archived by Al Jazeera Arabic, https://www.youtube.com/watch?v=1WPPAFA9ZJs.

50
See Daqqa's letter published in ʿArab 48, October 31, 2010, https://www.arab48.com//ثقافة-وفنون/نص/2010/10/31/رسالة-الأسير-وليد-دقة-في-اليوم-الأول-من-عامه-العشرين-في-الأسر!.
See also al-Shaikh, "Al-Makān al-Muwāzī," especially pages 197–200.

51
خالد جمعة، "قليل مما ستقول غزة عما قليل،" مجلة الدراسات الفلسطينية، العدد ١٣٧ (٢٠٢٤)، ص ٣١٩.

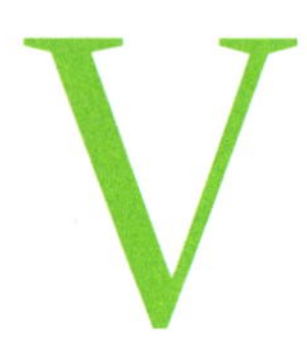

هاي المصطلحات جايبة دَوَرْنا
قد ما فتّشنا ودَوَّرْنا
عالعَمَية الضّو وَرْنا
احنا مش نَفْس الحكاي
بس كَماتْنا بنحسّ في بَرَكةْ
من يوم يومنا نقاوم، فبَرْكِي
اليوم تاريخنا يقتل الفَبْرَكِة
قبل بكرا اللّي جاي
جوّا الزمّن في كَمْشة طلق
عديم إحساس كان يرقص
شاف السما، ركض، انطلق
قلب عربي وحكى عليّ الطلاق
ما بعمري أرجع أطلع من هالولاي
احنا فأقوى مرحلة، فلا تكون سَلْبِيّ
هاي الخرايط خَرْطَت سَلْبِيْ
الفراغ صدى الدم سالْ بِيْهْ
كله مرسوم بعناي

المقاوَمة مِش رومانسيّات
هي ممارسة الرَفْض
ال لا الإيجابية
وطمأنة النّبض

To resist is to refuse to be quashed by the structural weight of Catastrophe, to rebuild your home even under incessant shelling. The steadfastness of Palestinians is awe-inducing, but we must not romanticize resistance and return. To do so is to give in to abstraction, to strip Palestine, and especially Gaza, of its material sacrifices. Abstraction is not only perpetuated by the "international community," but within Palestinian society as well, particularly the comprador class, who continue to portray Gaza in the negative, Othering its—our—people as Gazans (and not Palestinians from and within Palestine).[52] This Othering concedes to colonial lines, carving out Gaza as an external strip of abjection and condemnation. It is not as though Gaza is outside Palestine, but the deadly Zionist siege and its beneficiaries have relegated it as a distant, isolated place at both the discursive and physical level. As we near the twelfth month of genocide, it is clear that Gaza has also been politically externalized.

شعب صابر بالغصب. صدمة غزة قلب
شعبي في أضعف وأقوى حالاته بنفس الوقت
أَمّا المقاومة تضاعفت آخر ١٥٠ سنة فيوم واحد
ولا ظفر راح عالفاضي آخر ١٥٠ سنة ساحت

انتقام الأطفال تعبير طاهِر
دروع الإمّيات ضدّ الخونة طاهِر
كُلّ ما بِنشِدّ، أَضعافُه بِحاصِر
أَضعافُه بِذْبَح، رووس وخواصِر
بِشَتِّتوا الانتفاضة، بِشَتِّتوا المساطر
كابوسهُم رَجْعِتنا. فَبِقَتْلوا مَقابِر
في فرق بين متظاهِر ومتظاهِر
التّاني كَذّاب، والأوّل طاهِر

52
The majority of Gaza's population are actually descendents of refugees from coastal cities and towns north of Gaza, whom Zionist militias expelled in 1948.

Rewind to May 2021: following the colonial court decision to expel Palestinian families from the Jerusalem neighborhood of Sheikh Jarrah in favor of settlers, a people's uprising ignited across Palestine. It marked a brief but significant moment of social cohesion and political consciousness across colonial lines, particularly for those in the occupied interior who for the first time in decades, rose against their/our colonizer. Why then did this remarkable uprising against Zionist settler-colonialism, from the heart of Jerusalem to the territories occupied in 1948, and even momentarily in Ramallah after the Palestinian authority assassinated the cogent and principled oppositionist Nizar Banat, culminate in the bombing of Gaza? As we resisted our dispossession, why did we rally and chant "!يا غزة يالله مشان الله Oh Gaza, come on, for God's sake!]" expecting Gaza to intervene on behalf of Jerusalem?

أنا الوعي اللي بفلت وقت ما بده
هوية ضفة تستبده
إذا حدا من غزة سمعني بتغنوج، يا إمّا حيضحك يا إمّا حيكفر

Writing about Gaza in 2021 from Cairo's Tora Maximum Security Prison, Egyptian political dissident Alaa Abd El-Fattah probes: "does a captive have the right to ask for help from the besieged?"[53] Abd El-Fattah's question has gained urgency as we reckon with what it means to live in micro- and macro-prisons, to transcend material and ideological containments, and to actually do the cohering and congealing labor of solidarity and mobilization on all fronts. Regarding the axis of Gaza and Jerusalem, Odetallah underscores Gaza's role in defending Jerusalem and safeguarding Al-Aqsa—the physical and symbolic focal point of Palestine's anticolonial struggle—which, in its being taken for granted, has engendered a relationship not of solidarity, but of dependency.[54] The existential implications of this unidirectional dynamic are cumbersome—how can we define ourselves as a people given such nonreciprocal relationality? And what has conditioned this social equation where one faction incurs a much higher price for daring to exist beyond disavowal? "We have reached a stage where people are calling on Gaza to enter a fierce war," remarks Odetallah, "where hundreds and thousands of martyrs in Gaza will fall just to halt a settler parade."[55] This is not a critique of resistance, but of the dangerous dependency, indeed the expectation segments of our society have developed regarding Gaza's role as the exclusive resistance front for all of Palestine. The very plea for Gaza alone to mobilize and sacrifice itself for the sake of Jerusalem devalues the lives of our people in Gaza, including our freedom fighters who have yet to be grieved. It falls short of confronting the social acquiescence to a permanent "fact" of siege, let alone the periodic bombing of Gaza which has gone unabated for almost two decades.

بصرخوا عالكاميرا
بنتفرج زي أميرة
بعيدة فقلعة فجزيرة
والواقع بيننا ساعتين
نصنا بده ينبسط
زيح فيديو، هات كلب وقط
نشد بعض قالت الست
كبيرها نحطّها فاغنيتين
شطّحت وبطّحت
يحرّروها مش غلط
من هون لوقتها هات قطط
لا تلومنا يا غراب البين
بس نصنا التاني مرابط
عباب القرية حاطط
عصاية وضو مْشارط
يهجموا الأندال في الليل

As a colonial enterprise, Zionism requires division to maintain its rule; it needs to destroy the memory and possibility of a resistant indigenous collective. Rather than succumbing to this division, Gaza has consolidated a united front, bringing together diverse factions of Palestinian resistance, from Islamist to Marxist-Leninist, under the banner of the Joint Operations Room [الغرفة المشتركة لفصائل المقاومة]. It is true that the resistance is strongest and most centralized in Gaza, where it can operate with a level of freedom unmatched in the rest of Palestine. This is precisely the double

53
Alaa Abd El-Fattah, "Palestine on My Mind," *Mada Masr*, September 16, 2021, https://www.madamasr.com/en/2021/09/16/opinion/u/palestine-on-my-mind/.

54
Odetallah, "إيش عملت فينا الحرب على غزة؟.. مع الباحث خالد عودة الله" [What has the war on Gaza done to us? With researcher Khaled Odetallah], Quds Podcast, YouTube video, 1:19:18, April 24, 2024, https://www.youtube.com/watch?v=sfz0H5pzZ0g.

55
Odetallah, "What has the war on Gaza done to us?"

bind of anticolonial struggles: those who resist face the most heinous colonial violence because they are the most free. As Abd El-Fattah notes, "Gaza is besieged but it has not been taken captive, and the difference is enormous."[56] Within this difference, this negative, is the resistance.

The strategy of divide and conquer not only disproportionately targets certain factions of our society but also externalizes violence, making it appear distant and exceptional. Beneath this veneer of exceptionalism lies the very work of colonialism: isolating Gaza from Palestine and Palestinians from the world, stripping our struggle of its foundations, precluding political parallels and solidarity efforts, and extinguishing thousands of years of indigenous existence. The recourse to exception exonerates colonial brutality by using the suspension of law as a pretext for acts of violence that have always represented the rule. It is a strategy that preserves colonial law precisely by holding it in abeyance, managing liberal sensibilities, and rendering otherwise unacceptable violence rational and justifiable. In practice, the suspension of law does not only condone colonial transgressions and violations, but, as Palestinian legal scholar Wael Hallaq explained, "does so partly in the process of creating new international norms. In other words, so-called violations of the norm are re-created as norms."[57] This is how the supposedly exceptional bombing of al-Mamadani Hospital, for example, is restaged at al-Shifa, Kamal Adwan, Nasser, and the Indonesian hospitals, to name a few. At stake is the hardening of Gaza's exceptional status, wherein its siege and recurrent bombing (the colonial "state of emergency") are normalized and reproduced as acceptable forms of population control.

”هل الخوفَ مخيفٌ؟“[58]
أظنّ حَسَب
بس خوفِك أكيد بخوِّفني

56
Abd El-Fattah, 2021.

57
Wael Hallaq, *Restating Orientalism, A Critique of Modern Knowledge* (New York: Columbia University Press, 2018), 222.

58
نعمة حسن، ”هكذا نهدهد الحرب لتنام،“ مجلة الدراسات الفلسطينية، العدد ١٣٧ (٢٠٢٤)، ص ٣٢٣

VI

بغيروا نظرتهم لإلنا بكبسة كبّاسة
عِد للتلاتة
هُبْ
مِن خَطَر لَعَدَمُه
مِن معسكر لمخيّم
مِن فَلَحُه لعَمَرُه
مِن جماعة لَفَرْد
بِسلاسة
بِدهُم نفقد الأمل
الموضوع مش بس شَماتة
مش لازم نسمّيهم مرضى نفسيّين
هيك بنبرّئ الإنسان من النّجاسة
هُبْ
من اسم قرية لاسم مجزرة
من بشر لَمَبْشَرة
من سكني لأحمرة
ألوان إبادة

The coordinates of colonial governance precariously shift between life and death, collapsing any conjectured distinction between biopolitical and necropolitical management. Palestinian enclaves and refugee camps, residual and negated nonplaces, function as reservoirs of labor ("labor camps") under a Zionist regime of biopower. What the programmatic flexibility of the Palestinian enclave reveals is the expendability of Palestinian life, stripped down to bare existence; as Daqqa put it, "less than a people, but above physical extermination."[59] Writing fifteen years ago during his twenty-third year of imprisonment, Daqqa contended that "Palestinian enclaves are not temporary ghettos or stations where Palestinians are gathered before the 'final solution'— rather, they are the final solution [*al-ḥal al-nihāʾī* - الحل النهائي]."[60] He continued, "the aim of this solution is not mass extermination (genocide), but the extermination of the soul through a cultural and civilizational genocide."[61]

While Daqqa's statement might initially seem contradictory to the genocide ongoing in Gaza, it serves as a foil to understanding the variability of colonial machinations. The enclaves themselves are indeed the final solution, with the caveat that they shift and mutate in an attempt to retain control and delay the imminent collapse of the decaying colony. There is further insight to be mined from the first half of Daqqa's statement. Returning to the negational grammar of the colony, the word "final" [*nihāʾī*] in final solution [*al-ḥal al-nihāʾī*] derives from the same root as prohibition [the n-h-y tripartite]. This etymological foundation, as we already unraveled, is predicated on marking end points. The colonial aim is to set a limit and ultimately bring an end to Palestinian existence, compressing and constricting us to the point of suffocation. The terminal limit is also a conceptual inversion of the colony's expanding borders. As the colonial domain widens, the patches of land where Palestinians are confined contract. This deliberate encroachment facilitates the shift from biopower to necropower, conditioning us to the increasing permeability between life and death.

تعا عالي
ياما ياما مات
بس رجعت و جيت
بأناشيد

59
Daqqa, *Ṣahr al-Waʿī*, 30.

60
Daqqa, 32.

61
Daqqa, 32.

The value in Daqqa's point lies in its refusal to accommodate this fallacy, as the enclave encompasses both biopower and necropower under a single colonial principle, pushing towards the limit of Palestinian existence. Daqqa's recent martyrdom relays this illusion, as he was repeatedly denied release despite being diagnosed with a rare and aggressive type of bone marrow cancer. His case is not merely one of medical neglect but of systemic abuse, receiving the bare minimum treatment in sparse, controlled doses that ultimately led to a protracted and painful death. The colonial prison, operating as a "micro" enclave, represents the terminal limit for Palestinian prisoners, where every breath is caged and counted, hanging in delicate balance. Finally, the continued detention of Daqqa's corpse in colonial morgues serves as a grim testament to how the colony's bio- and necropolitical regimes cohere as one, holding Palestinians captives in both life and death.[62]

Discerning the mutability of the colonial project, that it is unfixed and can therefore come undone, is necessary to materializing its dissolution. Anthropologist and historian Ann Stoler posits that "a 'colony' as a political concept is not a place but a principle of managed mobilities, mobilizing and immobilizing populations according to a set of changing rules and hierarchies that order social kinds: those eligible for recruitment, for resettlement, for disposal, for aid, or for coerced labor, and those who are forcibly confined."[63] As a product of colony, the enclave follows this principle, controlling movement via permits and prohibitions, fragmenting and reshuffling populations, dispossessing the already dispossessed, and imprisoning and executing the unwieldy. The nonplace of the enclave adheres to the logic of the colony, fluctuating between prohibition and termination as it molds land into territory, camp, and prison. It is not simply a concentration of populations, but a strategic partitioning of bodies into more manageable units of restriction and control, both in life and in death. The land and its people are thus melted and molded anew to serve colonial objectives, whether for labor and production or for death and obliteration.

We reject the distinction between the regulation of life, meted out in droplets, and the administration of death, delivered in showers of bombs. The liberal constitution of the refugee camp as a charitable arrangement for the sheltering of the dispossessed is not at odds with the imperial infrastructure of the concentration camp. As Nasser Abourahme tells us, "These seemingly different 'types' were not separate analogues, but parts of the same whole."[64] The fact that Gaza's Nuseirat, Bureij, and Maghazi camps were host to a range of British imperial disciplinary practices (including military posts, police barracks, detention centers, and concentration camps) before being constituted as refugee camps in 1948 reveals that the enclave is neither exceptional nor haphazard. Rather, it is genealogically lodged to Empire, insidiously morphing to maintain its power. The penitential pasts of Palestine's enclaves and camps have subsequently been recycled and reproduced as benevolent presents of refuge. Imperialism, continually transforming yet never concealing itself, sits squarely within humanitarian aid and development projects, arrogantly manufacturing postcolonial illusions of progress as Zionism sets Palestine's camps ablaze. The false dichotomy between the biopolitics of humanitarianism and the necropolitics of genocide is especially laid bare in Gaza today, where "safety zones" function as death traps, rations become a lure for the slaughter of the starving,[65] a "humanitarian pier" serves as a launchpad for massacres, and aid trucks act as a Trojan Horse for further atrocities.[66]

62
While imprisoned, Daqqa wrote a play about the afterlife consciousness of a Palestinian martyr who awakens to find himself trapped in a refrigerator in an occupation prison morgue alongside other martyrs. The play reflects a poignant parallel to Daqqa's own posthumous captivity, acutely emphasizing the prevalence of this morbid colonial practice. See Daqqa, "Al-Shuhadā Ya'ūdūn ilā Ramallah" [The Martyrs Return to Ramallah] (Walid Daqqa Manuscript Archive, 2021). For an insightful discussion of the play, see Abdul-Rahim al-Shaikh's eponymous article in *Journal of Palestine Studies*, no. 133 (2023): 128–155.

63
Ann Laura Stoler, *Duress: Imperial Durabilities in Our Times* (Durham: Duke University Press, 2016), 117.

64
Nasser Abourahme, 279.

65
In reference to the Flour Massacre west of Gaza City on February 29, 2024, when Zionist colonial forces shot at starving Palestinians awaiting aid convoys, killing 118 and injuring 760.

66
massacre in Gaza's Nuseirat refugee camp, when Zionist soldiers infiltrated the camp by hiding in an aid convoy, then proceeded to open fire on displaced Palestinians before launching airstrikes on the camp, resulting in the deaths of at least 276 Palestinians and injuries of around 700. The massacre was facilitated by U.S. involvement, including intelligence support and the "scandalous" use of the Biden-funded "humanitarian pier"—a move that is, in fact, dogmatically consistent with U.S. foreign policy (read imperialism). To no Palestinian's surprise, the U.S. announced the dismantling of the pier shortly after the massacre, plainly showcasing the violent intent behind its construction.

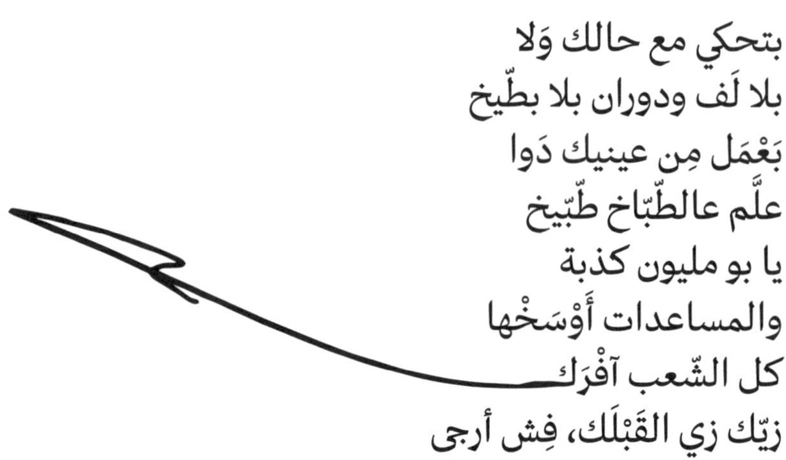

The transition from life to death, from land to prison, from people to populations, and from resistance to martyrdom highlights the pervasive and tenuous nature of colonial negation. Yet, the colony is also precariously perched on the edge. Just as land can be reduced to territory, it can also be restored. As Palestinian resistance has repeatedly demonstrated, the colonial limit is not impenetrable. The elasticity of the colonial border, its relentless expansion and insatiable greed for land make it especially prone to failure. When Mahmoud al-Ardah, one of the six imprisoned Palestinians who tunneled their way out of Gilboa Prison declared that “this monster is but an illusion of dust,” he affirmed the ephemerality of the Zionist colonial enterprise and imminence of Palestinian return. It is not as though al-Ardah, who uttered these words in court after his recapture, undermines the structural weight of colonialism—in fact, he was attacked and beaten by colonial officers as he spoke—but that he firmly refuses to be crushed under its burdensome heft. Remarkably, those in the negative, teetering on the perilously thin verge of death, believe most firmly in life and liberation.

While the hackneyed Zionist slogan “a land without a people for a people without a land” contrived a discursive vacuity, it has failed to materialize this emptiness at the physical level. In this “unpeopled” land every indigenous life is an excess, always already against the colonial script, spilling outside its borders, continually redacted, contained, and tightened. Our absence is marked by densely packed homes atop scarce and costly dunums, queues at checkpoints, overcrowded prisons, flooded processions of mourning and return, ever-concentrated camps, and rising birth rates which Zionism cites as it aborts entire genealogies. The enclave as the final solution has indeed become more restrictive and stifling. Yet, it has also been shattered, tunneled through, glided over, and dismantled. How swiftly those settlements in Gaza and Jenin collapsed and disappeared, their structural weight dissipating into dust,[67] as though they never were.

كلهم مستعمرين، من بيت إيل لتل أبيب
اصحكم تصدقوهم. والله مصيرهم رحيل
وأنا بغنّي من روحي. آه
هم حياخدوا روحي؟

The failure of the colonial project—its inability to actualize the fantasy of an unpeopled land—leaves it open and unbound, creating space, however minimal, for an otherwise. Despite its hollowing, the land continues to resist and sprout native life against invasive ecosystems, spawning beyond cartographic lines and marking the ruins of razed villages, as if to commemorate countless unknowable martyrs. Our portrait in the negative is still processing, the absented presence coming into focus, the soil reddening from purple to brown,[68] anticipating the return of our workers from their enslavers and our captured from their jailers, once the five geographies are sutured, the sixth destroyed, and self and kin are restored.

67
This is not to underestimate the scale of debris and waste deposited on indigenous land. After the resistance's triumph in 2005, the legions of military posts and settlements that once infested Gaza were razed by Zionist bulldozers to prevent Palestinians from ever using them, leaving behind their colonial rot and wreckage as retribution for Gaza's liberation. (Though, as we know, the primary reprisal came in the form of a siege). For more on the toxic residues of Empire, see Stoler's introduction to her edited volume *Imperial Debris: On Ruins and Ruination* (Durham: Duke University Press, 2013), 1–35.

68
Abbas and R. Abou-Rahme, *May amnesia*, 2021–.

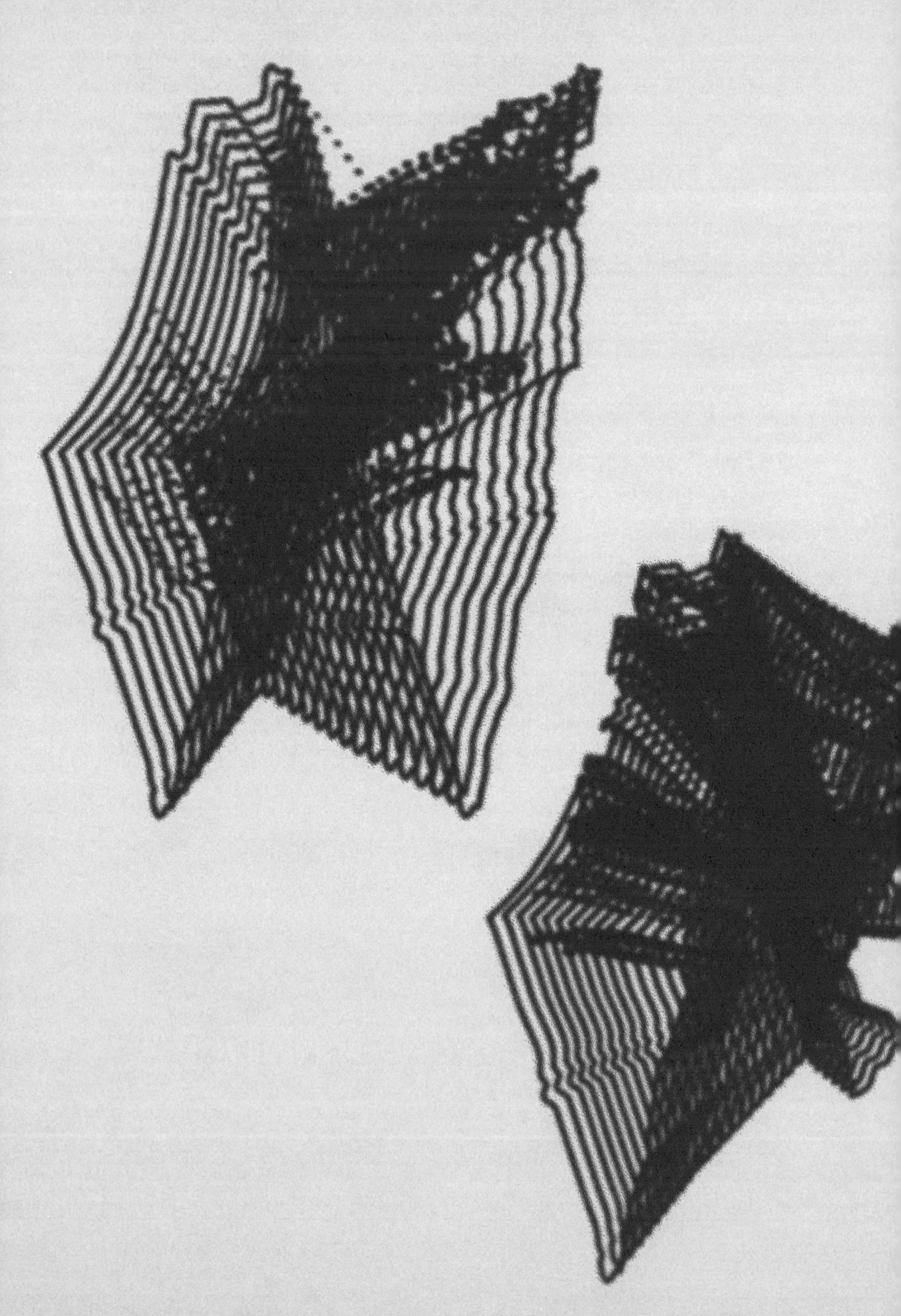

مقاومة بُنية النكبة في الناقص المسلوب

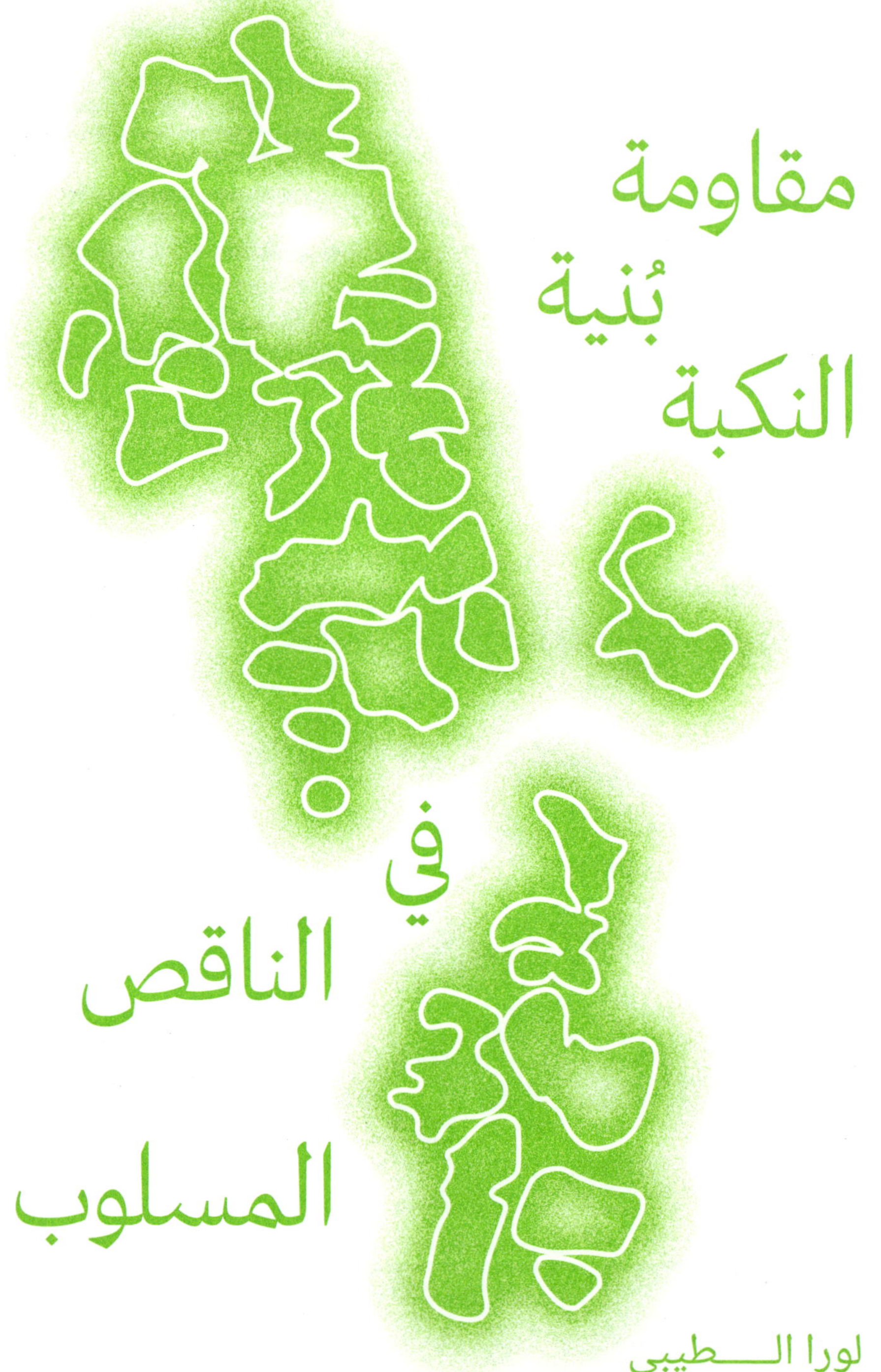

لورا الـــطيبي
و عمرو عامر

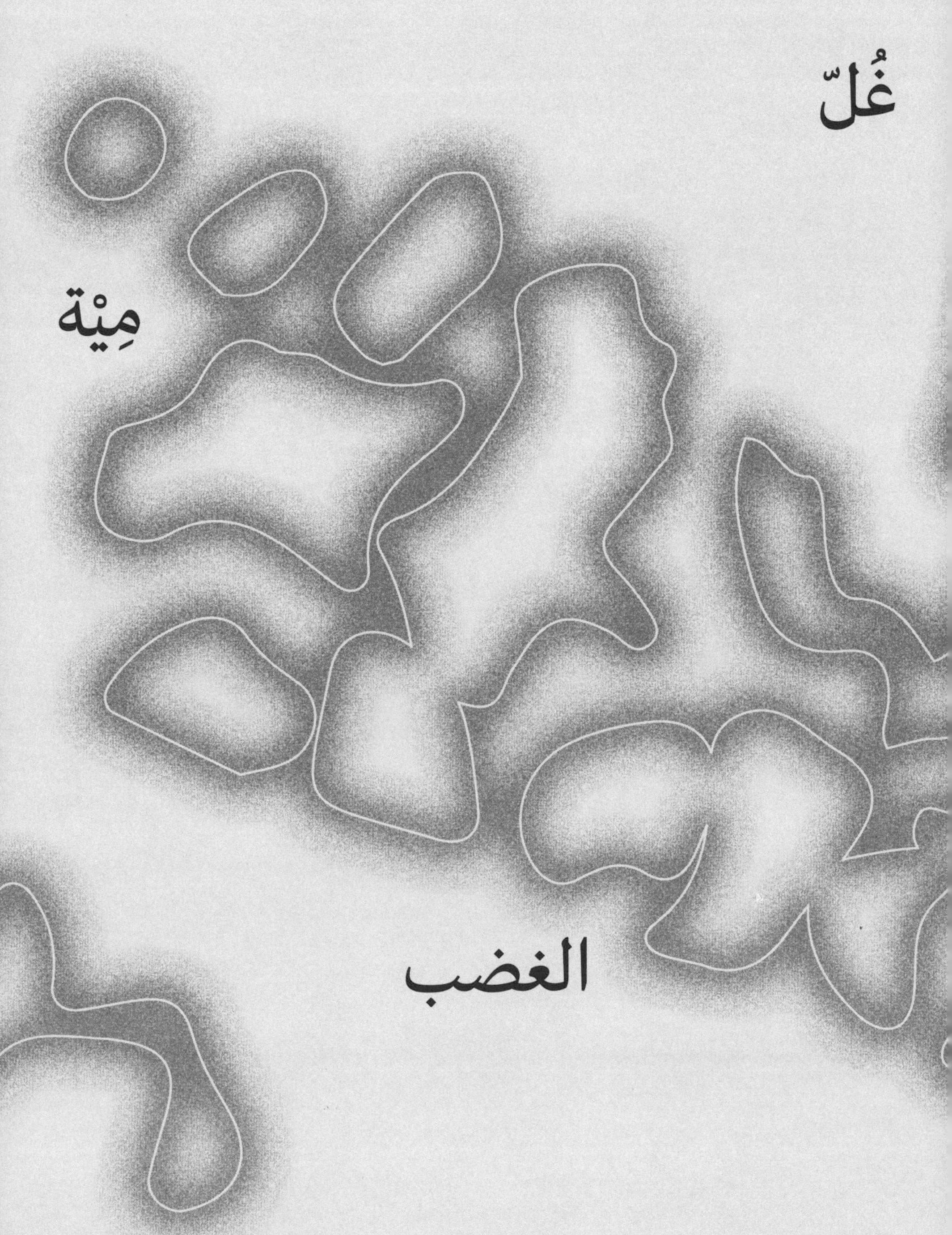
غُلّ
مِيْة
الغضب

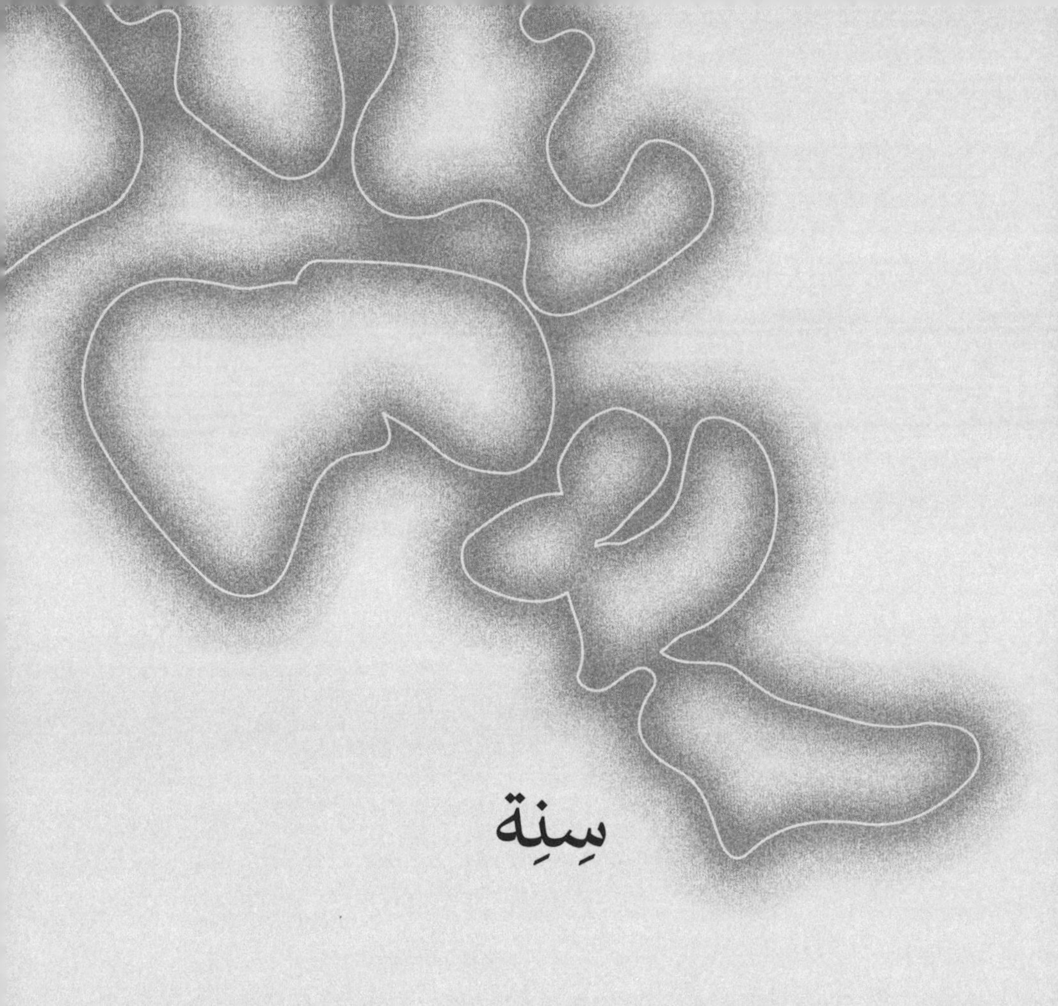

سِنِة

هذا

إلي

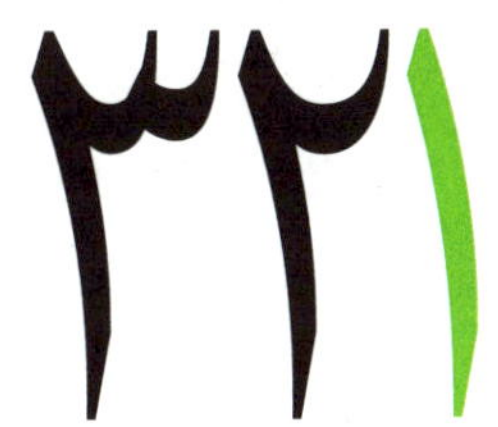

ما معنى أن تُقْتَلع الأرض من جذورها وبيئتها، وأن يُخْتَزَل نظامها البيئيّ، حتّى تُصبح بقعة مجرّدة من كافّة مقوّمات الحياة؟ وما مصير أهلها المنفيّين المهجّرين؟ ما الّذي سيدفعهم نحو عودتهم الحتميّة إلى أرضهم لغرس جذورهم فيها من جديد؟

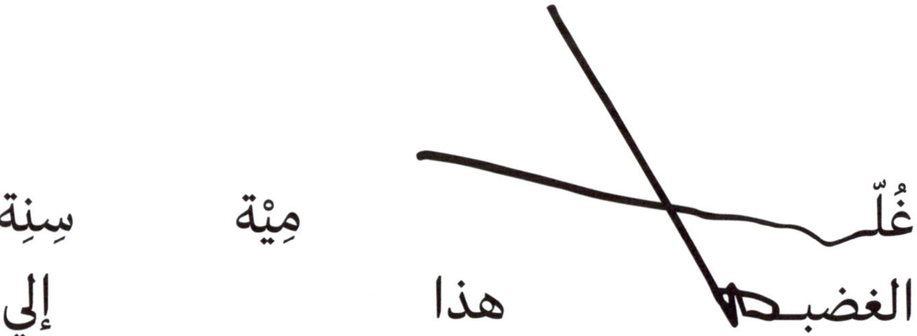

نقرأ النكبة الفلسطينيّة كسلسلة نفي تتراكم لتخلق غيابًا مهولًا على أرض مُزّقت. هذا هو التفريغ الماديّ والخطابيّ لفلسطين، إنكار علاقتنا بالأرض، تجريف محاصيلنا، تدمير ديارنا، تعطيل تقاليدنا وطقوسنا المتناغمة مع إيقاعها. بينما تتعرّض الأرض للتآكل التاريخيّ لأكثر من قرن، يمثّل عام ١٩٤٨ الخسارة الكارثيّة، وولادة النكبة بتبعاتها المتتالية. قدّم المؤرّخ الفلسطينيّ عارف العارف عنوان كتابه "نكبة بيت المقدس والفردوس المفقود" عام ١٩٥٦ قائلًا حول قرار التقسيم: "وكيف لا أسمّيه (النكبة)؟"، معقبًا "وقد نُكِبنا[١]". النكبة، كما عرّفها الإنتاج المعرفيّ الفلسطينيّ ليست حدثًا واحدًا، وإنّما هيكل مستمرّ، يستمدّ أصله الأيدولوجيّ من الاستعمار الأوروبّيّ، بينما تستند إليه الصهيونيّة، وتطبّقه بشكله الأكثر ضراوة ووحشيّة. لا يمكن حصر النكبة أو تقسيمها؛ فهي تتغلغل في الأرض، وتملأ الأجساد حتّى تفيض بالرفض والمقاومة، ضدّ ثِقَل هذا الاستعمار المترسّخ. فما الأشكال الّتي يتراءى لنا وَقْع النكبة من خلالها، وبأيّ مفردات سياسيّة؟

١
عارف العارف، النكبة: نكبة بيت المقدس والفردوس المفقود، ١٩٤٧-١٩٤٩، الجزء الأوّل (صيدا، لبنان: منشورات المكتبة العصريّة للطباعة والنشر، ١٩٥٦)، ص. ٣، كما تُرْجِم واقتُبِس في مقال جوزيف مسعد "العمل الثقافيّ لاستعادة فلسطين" [The Cultural Work of Recovering Palestine]، باوندري ٢ [*boundary 2*]، المجلّد ٤٢، العدد ٤ (٢٠١٥): ص.١٩٠-١٩١.راجعوا تحديدًا تمييز مسعد بين استخدام كلمة "catastrophe" المشتقّة من اليونانيّة والتي تعني "تحوّل مفاجئ"، وتُسْتَخدم غالبًا في سياق وصف الكوارث الطبيعيّة أو اختلال التوازن الكونيّ، واستخدامه للمصطلح العربيّ "النكبة"، الّذي يعبّر عن كارثة ناتجة عن الاستعمار الاستيطانيّ الصهيونيّ، ممّا جعل الفلسطينيّين "منكوبين".

اتْبَرّا من أبوه عالعَلَن
سَلَخوا بعض غمزة تمثيل
شجر جوّا العُش فاجأهم
"كيف ما كفّاكم تنكيل؟"
ما العُش مِش عُش
العُش هاد منجم
قَسّى جيل وَرا جيل وَرا جيل

في عملهما الفنّيّ المستمرّ "ليت النسيان لا يقبّلنا على الشفتين"، ينظر باسل عبّاس وروان أبو رحمة إلى "الناقص/ السلبيّ"، إذ يطرحانه كمفهوم جماليّ وسياسيّ ينبثق من الأرض - ولا تُعْتَبر الأرض هنا موقعًا للسلب فقط، وإنّما كيان متجدّد ينبت الحياة المتجذرة لمواجهة الدمار المتكرّر. ممارستهم الفنّيّة الحسّيّة لصناعة الأفلام تغمرنا في الأرض، وتجعلنا نتغلغل في التربة، وتحرّكنا مع النباتات حيث نتنفس عبر "مسامات هذا البحر وهذه الأرض التي وصفوها بالميّتة[٢]"، فتنبض الحياة التي تشهد عليها القرون، تحت طبقات من التعفّن الاستعماريّ، رابطةً الأسلاف بالأحياء. تمنح هذه الصيرورة الفرصة للتنفّس والتحرّر، خلافًا للوضع الراهن، وتفسح مجالًا لغيره. هذه النظريّة التي يطرحها كلّ من باسل وروان حول "الناقص" في السياق الفلسطينيّ، توفّر إطارًا لقراءة النكبة، ليس فقط كهيكل مستمرّ، وإنّما كشيءٍ يُخلخل ويحوّل تفكّكنا لنعود معًا من جديد.

ومع ذلك، قبل أن نلتفت إلى الاحتمال الآخر، يجب أوّلًا أن نواجه الثقل البنيويّ للنكبة، ونتعامل مع عنف سلبها الفعليّ. بشكل رئيسيّ، تُنكر الصهيونيّة وجود الفلسطينيّين، وتعمل على "إخفائهم"، فتجعلنا مجرّد عرب ينبغي أن نتماهى في أيّ دولة مجاورة، نكون فيها عربًا بدلًا من فلسطينيّين مرتبطين بالأرض منذ قرون. تُخْضِع النكبة الزمن لعنفها المتناوب، تشوّه التاريخ، وتقمع الماضي الّذي يستحضر الصدمة في أجسادنا مع كلّ حدث جديد.

٢
باسل عبّاس وروان أبو رحمة، "ليت النسيان لا يُقَبّلنا على الشفتين"، ٢٠٢١–، https://mayamnesia.com/.

يتطلّب نفينا وإخفاؤنا استردادًا أرشيفيًّا، وبحثًا في قوّة أدلّة الماضي لإثبات الوجود الأزليّ للفلسطينيّين على هذه الأرض. نستدعي الصور الفوتوغرافيّة، سندات تسجيل الأراضي، جوازات السفر "الانتدابيّة"، وغيرها من ملحقات الحداثة البرجوازيّة لنقول: "انظروا، كنّا فيما مضى حداثيّين!"[٣]، فاعتَرِفوا بنا. لكن، عزّزت السلطة المؤسّسيّة تعريفها الموجز للحقيقة من خلال هذه الأدلّة الإثباتيّة، أعادت صياغة الوجود الفلسطينيّ ليكون مشروطًا ومقرونًا بوجود الدولة[٤]، إذ يُعَاد تعريف الارتباط بالأرض من خلال إطار الانتماء إلى الدولة القوميّة، والّذي يُقاس بحمل الجنسيّة، ممّا يشكّل لغطًا كبيرًا بين الدولة ومفهوم التحرير[٥].

شو دَرّى سماواتنا
هَيْ فتافيت مَحّاي
هَي غطاية مجاري
هَي فِطرة غُنّاي
شو دَرّى سماواتنا
الإثبات مَضْيَعَة
التّصحيح غَلَط
غلَطة مْقَطَّعة
شو دَرّى سماواتنا

٣
غُرَيب طوقان، حداثات متنوّعة: موادّ لدراسة حداثة فلسطينيّة، ترجمة آلاء يونس (برلين: دار نشر شتيرنبرغ، ٢٠١٧)، ص ٣٨.

٤
كما قالت جولدا مائير في تصريحها: "لم يكن هناك شيء اسمه فلسطينيّون. متى كان ثمّة شعب فلسطينيّ مستقلّ بدولة فلسطينيّة؟ كانت جنوب سوريا قبل الحرب العالميّة الأولى، ثمّ أصبحت فلسطين بما في ذلك الأردنّ. لم يكن الأمر كما لو أنّه كان هناك شعب فلسطينيّ في فلسطين، وجئنا وأخرجناهم منها، وأخذنا بلدهم منهم. لم يكن لهم وجود". فرانك جايلز، "جولدا مائير: 'من يمكنه لوم إسرائيل؟'"، صنداي تايمز [Sunday Times]، ١٥ تمّوز ١٩٦٩.

٥
كما هو الحال في اتّفاقيّة أوسلو، والتي تُعَدّ تضحية واضحة بالتحرير دفاعًا عن هيكل الدولة الرمزيّ.

لم يعد جوهر حضورنا المغيّب ما نشير إليه في سندات الملكيّة، أو الصور التاريخيّة، أو بطاقات الهويّة، بل أصبح في الأرض نفسها؛ تلك الأرض الّتي دُمّرت وأُخْلِيت من سكّانها، الشاهدة على نكبتنا وتاريخنا المدفون، فهي ليست محلّ أثرنا فحسب، وإنّما ترمز إلى المحاولات الأبديّة لمحوه كلّيًّا. كيف يمكننا تصوير هذه الأرض وفقدانها؟ عندما تُجَزّأ وتفرّغ من معناها، أين يذهب تاريخها؟ هذه الصورة للفقدان، للحضور المغيّب والنكبة، تتمثّل في الحيّز السالب:

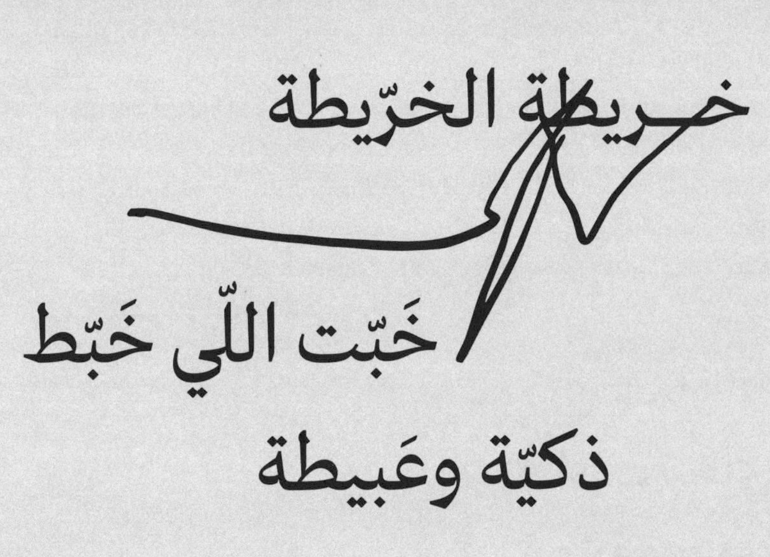

خريطة الخرّيطة

خَبّت اللّي خَبّط

ذكيّة وعَبيطة

سَلْبَت وْصَلْبت

ضيق النفس

هون صار عادات وتقاليد

وما فش حدا مواطن

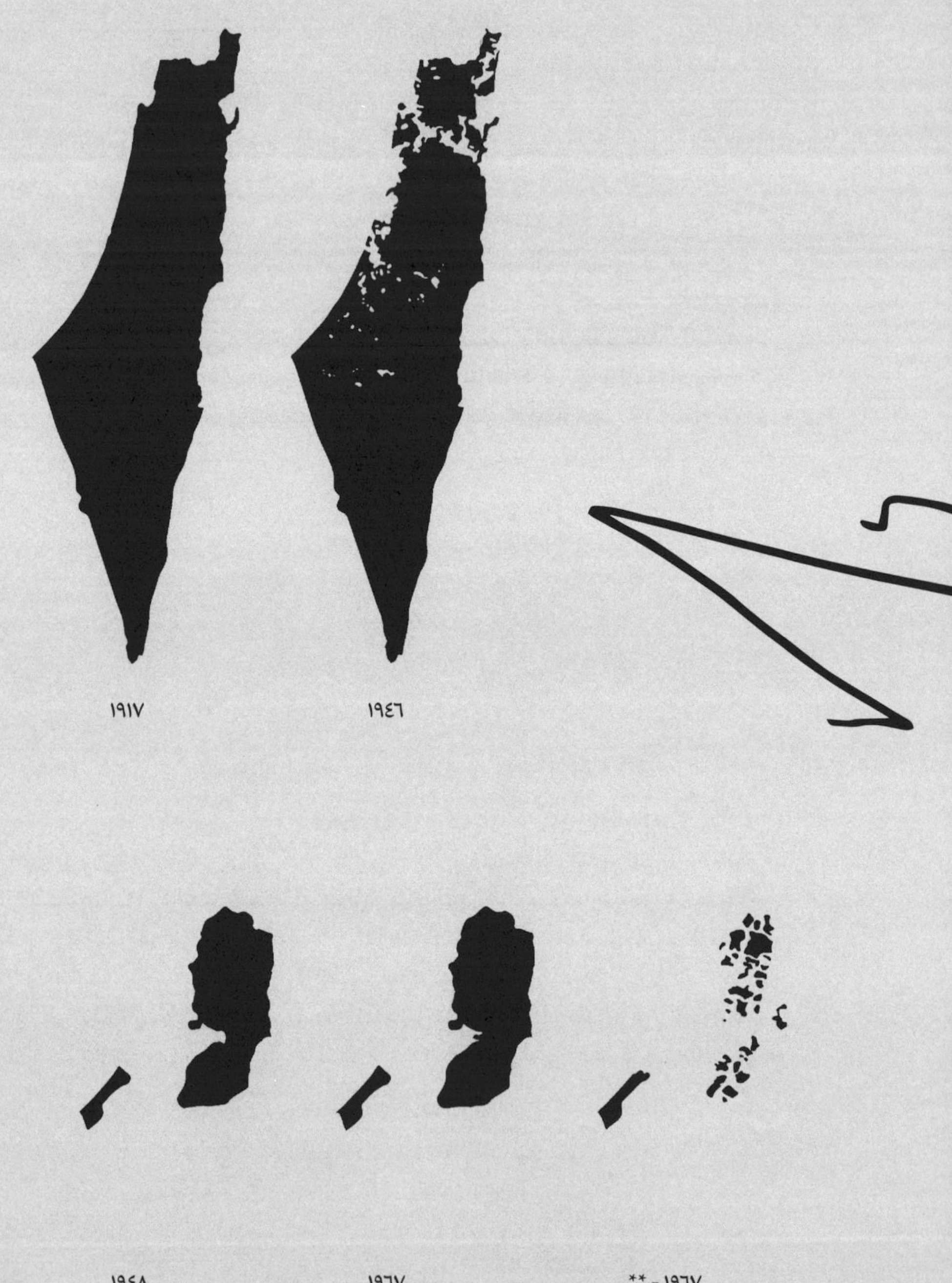
١٩١٧
١٩٤٦
١٩٤٨
١٩٦٧
١٩٦٧ - **

ليست الصورة للأرض بحدّ ذاتها، بل لمناطق[٦] تنكمش وتضيق وتختنق. إنّها تلخيص ملائم للخسارة، تُسَطَّح تمامًا في خرائط تعكس تلخيص اللغة الاستعماريّة للقضيّة، في دائرة مفرغة من المطالبات والمعاهدات، فتختزل وجود فلسطين في بيان سايكس بيكو المخادع، وبعض المستوطنات الساحليّة المتفرّقة. إنّها بداية العزل والتجريد، وتحويل أرضنا إلى مناطق، وشعبنا إلى سكّان. تطمئننا هذه الخريطة أنّ الأمور كانت بخير في ذلك الوقت، عندما كانت الأرض لا تزال تسمّى فلسطين. ولكنّ تعلّقنا بالخارطة الانتدابية عاطفيًا يجعلنا نتجاوز حقيقة الاحتلال البريطانيّ الدمويّ ودوره في دعم الاستيطان اليهوديّ الاستعماريّ، كما يجعلنا نتجاهل حقيقة أنّ الغرب قسّم أراضينا إلى مناطق وحدود مصطنعة أطلق عليها اسم "الشّرق الأوسط" (نسبة إلى أوروبا بالطبع). يقال إنّ فلسطين كانت هادئة قبل عام ١٩٤٨، خالية من الإقطاعيّين الّذين تآمروا مع المستعمرين، وساهموا في تسريع مصادرة أراضي العاملين. تُضفي هذه الصورة طابعًا من الرخاء على فلسطين متمثّلًا ببساتين برتقالها الخصبة، لتنأى بها عن واقع استغلال الطبقة العاملة الأصلانيّة.

ظَلَمِت يلّلي حَكَمِت عالأَبطـــال بالإعدام
فؤاد والزير والــــجمجوم راحوا غْـــدام
واللّهِ من حين مـــا قرّ الـــقرار بِعْدام
وانا مْـــقَرَّحِ الجِفِن من كثر البكـا ونـواح[٧]

هذا النموذج المثاليّ المفرغ من أيّ نضال ثوريّ يهدّدنا، ويمنحنا شعورًا زائفًا بالأمان، والّذي مهّد الطريق لحدوث النكبة عام ١٩٤٨: طُرِد أكثر من نصف الشعب الفلسطينيّ على يد الميليشيات الصهيونيّة. إذ تفتّتت هذه الأرض المتماسكة وتجزّأت، وهُجّر شعبُها إلى مناطق مقسّمة عسكريًا، ثمّ استئصِل الوجود الفلسطينيّ من الخرائط كمساحات فارغة في هذا الحيّز السالب— بقعة محاصرة في الشرق وشريط ساحليّ

٦
تقدّم سامرة إسمير تمييزًا هامًّا بين مصطلح الأرض والمنطقة، مشيرة إلى أنّ المنطقة/ الإقليم هو تصنيف استعماريّ قانونيّ: "فإن آلة المحو الإسرائيلية لا تكتفي باستهداف سكن الفلسطيني في **الأرض** التي، ومنذ عدة عقود، صنّفتها هذه الآلة، **بفعل قانونيّ**، إقليمًا إسرائيليًّا" [التشديد مضاف]. سامرة إسمير، "إرشادات غزّة: عن نهاية الحكم الاستعماريّ"، ترجمة عبد الرحيم الشيخ، مجلّة الدراسات الفلسطينيّة، العدد ١٣٧ (٢٠٢٣)، ص ٥.

٧
قصيدة لفهد الجلبوش، الّذي كان يعمل فرّانًا، كُتِبَت في أعقاب إعدام المقاومين الشهداء؛ محمّد خليل أبو جمجوم وعطا الزير وفؤاد حجازي. انظروا مقال إياد معلوف، "«من سجن عكّا»: كيف تفاعلت صحف فلسطين مع إعدام المناضلين الثلاثة؟"، موقع عرب ٤٨، ٢٠٢١. https://www.arab٤٨.com//فسحة/ورق/آخر/٢٠٢١/٠٩/٠٨/-من-سجن-عكا--كيف-تفاعلت-صحف-فلسطين-مع-إعدام-المناضلين-الثلاثة.

ضيّق في الجنوب الغربيّ، تُدار من قبل الملكيّتين اللّتين أنشأهما البريطانيّون في الأردنّ (الضفّة الشرقيّة) ومصر. بعد أن نُفينا إلى الهوامش، حُدِّدْنا وقُيِّدْنا بما يسمّى الخطّ الأخضر، الّذي سال حبره حتّى وصل إلى أطراف المناطق الّتي تزداد ضيقًا مع الوقت.

يتمّ القضاء على القرى والمدن والمناطق بأكملها لتمهيد الطريق للبنية التحتيّة الاستيطانيّة، إذ ينتج عن ذلك دمار تضاريسيّ ومحو تاريخيّ. يُعَدّ استبدال الأسماء الأصليّة للأماكن بأسماء عبريّة توراتيّة أجنبيّة جزءًا أساسيًّا من هذه العمليّة، والّتي تُعْتَبر مهمّة استعماريّة بدأها الأوروبيّون البروتستانت في منتصف القرن التاسع عشر، ثمّ تبنّاها لاحقًا المستوطنون الصهاينة[٨]. تتعدّى حملة إعادة التسمية فكرة التغيير الشكليّ؛ إذ تمثّل تحويلًا أيديولوجيًّا يعيد تشكيل الأرض على أنّها يهوديّة أصيلة و"مستردّة" من "ورثتها الشرقيّين الزائفين". في سعيه إلى المحو، قد يُرسّخ الاستعمار الاستيطانيّ أسماء الأماكن الأصليّة، ليس باعتبارها مواقع تاريخ أو تقاليد، بل كدلالة على المجازر. فماذا نعرف عن الطنطورة ودير ياسين وقبيا وكفر قاسم وصبرا وشاتيلا غير المجازر التي ارتُكبت في حق أهاليها؟ رفح وخان يونس وبيت لاهيا وجباليا يطرحون السؤال المروّع: أيّ مجزرة؟ نستطيع كشف حقيقة المنطق الوحشيّ للاستعمار من خلال هذا التناقض؛ إذ تُحوّل المجازر المتكرّرة هذه الأماكن إلى مناطق نعتاد فيها الموت، لتتحوّل بذلك إلى اللا-مكان، وبالتّالي، يُقْضَى على كلّ ما يميّزها، من عادات ولهجات أهلها الّتي تحمل في طيّاتها آلاف السنوات من التاريخ. لا تزيد الفظاعات المقترفة من حصيلة العنف فقط، بل تمحو ذكرى المجازر الّتي سبقتها، صانعة بذلك دورة موت لم نعهدها أبدًا. ونتيجة لذلك، نتعلّم جغرافيّتنا ويترسّخ إحساسنا بالمكان من خلال تاريخ كامل من الدمار والسلب. نحفر أسماء الشهداء الفلسطينيّين في اللامكان، ويصبحون الحاضر المغيّب في هذا الحيّز السالب. لكن، كيف يمكن للغة الجغرافيا المسطّحة أن تعبّر عن العبء العاطفيّ لهذه المجازر؟ وأين يمكن أن نحدّد في هذه الصورة الخطّيّة للنكبة نوبات القتل والذبح الّتي لا تتوقّف؟

٨
في عام ١٨٦٥، أُنْشِئ صندوق استكشاف فلسطين تحت الإدارة البريطانيّة كجزء من مشروع استعماريّ، يهدف إلى رسم الخرائط وإعادة تسمية فلسطين. لم يقتصر هذا المشروع الإمبرياليّ على تغيير أسماء المواقع، بل تضمّن أيضًا إعادة كتابة التاريخ واستغلاله من خلال الحفريّات الأثريّة. لمزيد من التفاصيل حول هذا الصندوق، يمكنك مراجعة مجلّتهم المحكّمة "فلسطين إكسبلوريشن كوارترلي" الّتي تأسّست في العام نفسه. وفي حال اهتمامك بمعرفة المزيد حول استمراريّة وتوسّع هذا المشروع الاستعماريّ البريطانيّ من قِبَل الحركة الصهيونيّة، يمكنك قراءة كتاب ناديا أبو الحاجّ "حقائق على الأرض: الممارسة الأثريّة وتشكيل الهويّة الإقليميّة في المجتمع الإسرائيليّ" (شيكاغو: جامعة شيكاغو، ٢٠٠١).

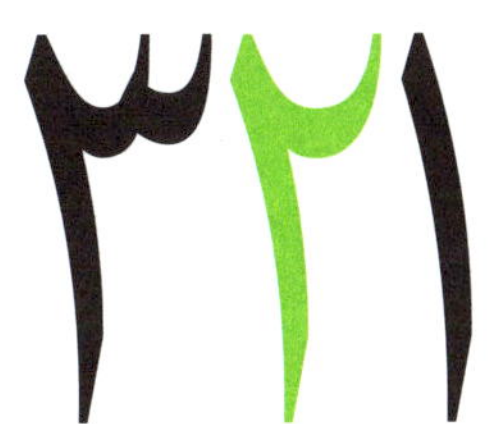

أن تكون
حيث أنت
أن تكون
حيث لا ينبغي أن تكون
...
نجد أنفسنا في النقص[٩]

كم من جنّة في البلاد

كم من جنّة

كمّل جمّع الشباب

كمّل جمّع

كانّي انشلّيت الإحساس

كانّي انشلّيت

مش زابطة نعيش

مش زابطة نعيش

من منظور المستعمِر، يتواجد السكّان الأصليّون دائمًا في السالب المنقوص، إذ يظهرون كقمع ملحوظ. نظر ناصر أبو رحمة إلى ذلك بوصفه "النفي الاستيطانيّ" (settler negation)، موضّحًا: "معنى النفي لا يتوقّف على تدمير الشيء، ولا كما تعرّفه القواميس برفض الوجود، إنّما يرتبط بكلا المعنَيَيْن، ولكنّه يختلف عنهما أيضًا، كما نستطيع تمييزه عن الحجب والإنكار. إنّ النفي رفض وجود شيء ما، مع التسليم بوجوده الفعلي[١٠]".

أَيا مكانا، هَيْنا فكلامَك واقف مع إنّي مِش موجود صافن في ابني المِش مولود تحت قصف الكذبة

٩
باسل عبّاس وروان أبو رحمة، ليت النسيان، نيسان - أيّار، ٢٠٢١.

١٠
ناصر أبو رحمة، "تحت الركام: المخيّم، المستعمرة، فلسطين" [Beneath the Concrete: Camp, Colony, Palestine]، رسالة دكتوراه (جامعة كولومبيا، ٢٠١٩)، ٢٢٦-٢٢٧.

في ظلّ تأكيد النفي الاستيطانيّ على عدم وجود السكّان الأصليّين، يعترف المستعمِر ضمنيًا بوجودهم، حتّى لو كان هذا الوجود هامشيًا، إذ إنّ مفردات النفي تنصّ بالضرورة على اقترانه ولو لغويًا بالمضطهدين؛ عند الحديث عنهم، وحتّى لو كان ذلك في الحيّز السالب. يرافق مفهوم *النّفي* مفهومًا ثانيًا، وهو *النهي*. يشمل النفي كافّة الأزمنة، ممّا يعزّز غيابًا وجوديًا شاملًا (لم يكن/ لا يوجد/ لن يكون هناك شيء اسمه فلسطين)، بينما النهي يقتصر فقط على الزمن المضارع/ الحاضر، إذ يُصْدِر الأوامر ضدّ فعل يحدث ويستمرّ بالحدوث (لا تسمّها فلسطين، لا تعش كفلسطينيّ، وببساطة لا تكن). يكشف هذا التفاعل بين النفي والنهي عن تناقض عميق: إذ يُعامَل الفلسطينيّون على أنّهم في خانة من اللاوجود، بينما يُمْنَعون من الوجود في اللحظة نفسها. لكن، كيف يمكن منع كيان يُفْتَرض أنّه غير موجود من الأساس؟

بِعْ عينُه **هاد مِش أنا**

مِش أرض هاي **أكيد هاي مِش سما**

يقدّم لنا مصطلحا النفي والنهي إطارًا أنطولوجيًا/ وجوديًا لمحو الفلسطينيّين وسلب أراضيهم. تنتمي كلمة النفي إلى الجذر *(نَفَى)*، ولها معنيّان أساسيّان ومتشابكان؛ الأوّل مرتبط بالإنكار والرفض والسلب، والثاني مرتبط بالطرد والإبعاد. يمكن قراءة التهجير الكارثيّ للفلسطينيّين على أنّه نفي للذات؛ إذ إنّ إبعادهم وطردهم من أرضهم هو بالضرورة إبعادهم عن أنفسهم. وإذا عدنا إلى الجذر نفسه، نَفَى، فإنّ (المنفيّين) ليسوا من أُبعِدوا عن الأرض فقط، وإنّما من تعرّضوا للسلب الوجوديّ والإنكار أيضًا، وبذلك، يخضع المنفيّون إلى عنف مضاعف؛ الإبعاد والطرد على المستوى الماديّ، والسلب على المستوى الوجوديّ. وبالمثل، يُشير مصطلح المنفى إلى المكان الفعليّ البعيد عن الأرض، كما يشير إلى هذا الحيّز السالب، وهو بهذه الحالة، أيّ مكان عدا فلسطين.

فِش اجرين فِش ايدين فِش مُخّ فِش شي

فِش منطق فِش اخت فِش في

أنا مَسْكة اللّحن، أنا السّالب. أنا فَلْتة عاللّحن، أنا السّالب.

السّالب بشلّك، هيك بتحكي الأسطورة

السّالب بشلّك، هيك بتحكي العصفورة

يُشتَقّ النّهيُ من الجذر *(نَهَى)*، والّذي يعني حَظَرَ أو مَنَعَ أو وَضَعَ حدًّا أو نهاية لشيء ما، وعادة ما يُستَخدم في سياق القيم والأخلاق. بينما تستخدم الـ (لا الناهية) وهي أداة النهي، لتعطي أوامر قاطعة بعدم حدوث الفعل. ونستطيع اشتقاق الفعل أنهى من الجذر نفسه أيضًا، والّذي يعني تصفيةً أو إتمامًا أو إيقافًا بشكل كامل، إذ تُشير عمليّة الإنهاء إلى أكثر من مجرّد وضع حدّ، وإنّما ضمان تحقيق هذا الحدّ وتنفيذه إلى أن ينتهي الأمر تمامًا. يعتمد مصطلحا النهي والإتمام على تعريف الحدود وفرضها، سواء كان ذلك متمثّلًا بعائق فوريّ أو نقطة نهاية، ويمكننا مدّ هذا المفهوم اللغويّ ليصل إلى مستواه الماديّ، فالنهايات لغويًا ورياضيًا تعني الحدّ، وما الحدود إلّا نقاط تفتيش وحواجز وجدران وحصار يتلو حصارًا لوجودنا. تضع اللا الناهية -والّتي نرى تمثّلاتها في

أساليب القمع والمنع- حدًا قاطعًا لإنهاء الوجود. وبينما تعتبر الحواجز الماديّة الوسيلة لإنهاء وجودنا، فإنّها، وفي الوقت نفسه، تعترف به وتشهد عليه؛ وكما هو الحال في مفردات النفي الّذي تحدّثنا عنه أعلاه، تفشل عمليّة الإنكار الوجوديّ (اللاوجود)، من خلال الاعتراف بوجود فلسطينيّ يجب حظره وإنهاؤه.

في شمال شرق داخل الخارج الغربِي المشتّت
أنا أكتر، بس أنقص، من محبوس بِتْفَتْفَت
وما في أفخر منّي حاليًّا عاللّي نبّت
اقطعوا نصّ الوقت من قِشْرُه
من خِشْنُه
مش فارقة. حتّى لو فَرْقَت

أن ترى فلسطين في الحيّز السالب، يعني أيضًا أن تشهد كلّ العنف الممتدّ لسياسات القمع والمحو، إذ تتبلور صورة موتنا ببطء أمام أعيننا. ففي صورة النكبة هذه، نستدلّ على العنف الاستعماريّ من خلال الغياب، إذ يكمن في الحيّز الناقص، وفي سلب الأرض وشعبها[١١]. تُعاد قَوْلَبة وجودنا المستمرّ قانونيًا في معانٍ عديدة على أنّنا "الحاضرون الغائبون"، إذ نُوصَف بـ"لاجئين وبلا جنسيّة ومتسلّلين وإرهابيّين ومُقيمين مؤقّتين". بالمختصر، نصبح لا-شعبًا. في هذا الفراغ الناقص، نحن لا نسكن أرضًا، بل **اتّجاهًا** (إذ سمّيت الضفّة الغربيّة نسبة إلى النهر الّذي تقع على ضفّته الأخرى مملكة إمبرياليّة المنشأ)، و**قطاعًا** (إذ تضاءلت مساحة أرض غزّة، وتفتّتت إلى أن أصبحت شقًّا ساحليًّا)؛ و**نصفًا** (إذ قُسِمت القدس إلى نصفين)؛ و**زمنًا** (إذ يُشار لما تبقّى من فلسطين نسبة للزمن المعلّق عند نكبة ١٩٤٨)؛ و**خارجًا** (نسبة للمنفيّين المهجّرين، بدءًا من مخيّمات اللاجئين المتناثرة في سوريا ولبنان والأردنّ، والممتدّة في أرجاء العالم)، أمّا الجغرافيا السادسة، كما أشار إليها الباحث الفلسطينيّ عبد الرحيم الشيخ، فهي سجون الاحتلال الصهيونيّ[١٢]".

١١
باسل عبّاس وروان أبو رحمة، ٢٠٢١.

١٢
عبد الرحيم الشيخ، "المكان الموازي: رسم الزمن في فكر وليد دقّة"، مؤسّسة الدراسات الفلسطينيّة، العدد ١٣٥ (٢٠٢٣): ٢٠٤-٢٠٥. انظروا أيضًا سلسلة الندوات الّتي قدّمها الشيخ مع قادة الحركة الوطنيّة الفلسطينيّة الأسرى: مروان البرغوثي، وليد دقّة، عبد الرزّاق فرّاج، عبد الناصر عيسى، وجدي جودة، باسم خندقجي، وثابت مرداوي، "ندوة الحركة الفلسطينيّة الأسيرة: الجغرافيا السادسة"، مؤسّسة الدراسات الفلسطينيّة، العدد ١٢٨ (٢٠٢١): ٩-٥٩.

بتعمل اشي، بعاقبوا الكلّ
ليبطلوا كلّ
خطّة قديمة لَيْرَبّوا الضّوء
مِش لازم نجمّل الواقع
شَلّحوا وشَوَّهوا العايش والمَيّت
فش غير في "دثّريني" جمال في اللّجوء
تشويه نفسي
وين ما كنّا
ما احنا وين ما كنا
ذنبنا بسوق
حتّى الأسرى بحسّوا بذَنْب
الزنزانة منفى
جوّاتها كمان منفى
وليد شَرَح انتصارُه
بفكّر في اللي حكاه وبَحاوِل أروق
اللّه يرحمه

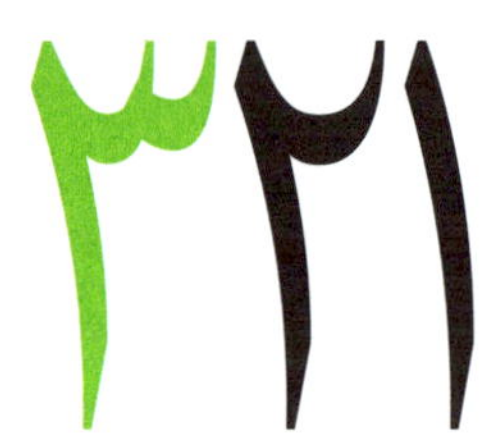

كتب الشهيد المثقّف وليد دقّة، وهو أسير في سجن جلبوع، عام ٢٠٠٩ عن سجون الاحتلال-الجغرافيا السادسة- أنّها نموذجٌ مصغّرٌ لفلسطين تعكس التشظّي الاستعماريّ للأرض[١٣]. يقع سجن جلبوع وراء الجدار الاستعماريّ وسلسلة جبال فقوعة (قضاء جنين)، حيث تُستغلّ التضاريس الطبيعيّة كحدود، إذ يُخَصّص هذا السجن للفلسطينيّين من شمال الضفّة الغربيّة، وتحديدًا من طولكرم، نابلس، وجنين، مع أقسام لأولئك القادمين من القدس ومناطق ١٩٤٨. وصف دقّة سجن جلبوع وغيره من السجون الاستعماريّة بأنّها سجون صغيرة داخل السجن الأكبر: فلسطين المستعمرة. في السجن الصغير، كما هو الحال في فلسطين بأكملها، يخضع الفلسطينيّون للفصل القسريّ في عنابر وزنازين تعكس تقسيم الأرض[١٤]. على الرغم من الاستخدام الدارج لمصطلح الفصل العنصريّ (الأبارتايد) لوصف القضيّة الفلسطينيّة، أشار وليد دقّة إلى عدم صحّة استخدامه في التعبير عن الشرط الاستعماريّ للوجود الفلسطينيّ. يدلّ معنى مصطلح الأبارتايد إلى الفصل العرقيّ بين "اليهود" و"العرب[١٥]" فقط، وبالتالي يغفل كمصطلح ويحجب فرص الفهم الحقيقيّ لنتائج الهندسة الصهيونيّة للفصل بين الفلسطينيّين أنفسهم. نرى في طرح دقّة ارتكازًا على التقسيم الجغرافيّ بدلًا من العرقيّ، والّذي يؤكّد مركزيّة عمليّة إعادة قولبة فلسطين كسجن كبير في نطاق المشروع الاستعماريّ. تستمرّ في الجغرافيا السادسة إعادة توزيع الأسرى الفلسطينيّين وعزلهم؛ هذا العزل الّذي عرّفه

١٣
وليد نمر دقّة، صهر الوعي، أو في إعادة تعريف التعذيب (بيروت: الدار العربيّة للعلوم ناشرون، ٢٠١٠).

١٤
دقّة، صهر الوعي، ص٣٢.

١٥
التميز الحادّ بين "اليهوديّ" و"العربيّ"، الّذي ينكر وجود اليهود العرب، تمّ إنشاؤه استعماريًّا قبل وجود أيّ بنية تحتيّة للفصل العنصريّ. كما يذكرنا محمود ممداني، أنّ الفصل العنصريّ قد قُدِّم كحلّ—وأعيد تغليفه دبلوماسيًّا في "حلّ الدولتين"—بدلًا من اعتباره مشكلة. محمود ممداني، "إدوارد سعيد والقضيّة الفلسطين" ندوة أكاديميّة، جامعة كولومبيا، نيويورك، ٢٦ نيسان ٢٠٢٤.

دقّة بالترحيلات والتنقيلات[16]، يعكس الاستراتيجيّات الأساسيّة الّتي تتبعها الصهيونيّة في نفي وتهجير الفلسطينيّيين[17]. تجسّد هذه الحالة من الانفصال والاغتراب تجزئة فلسطين ذاتها - من الكلّ الجمعيّ إلى الجسد المفكّك، ومن الشعب المتماسك إلى أفراد معزولين. يؤكّد وصف دقّة على إجراءات النفي والإبعاد داخل نظام السجون، ونتساءل هنا: مِنَ الجغرافيا السادسة، إلى أين يمكننا الذهاب؟

حاسس حالي فكيس نايلون
بِدَربونا نعيش بفُقاعات أمنية زي كيث دايتون[18]

مُختَبَرْ ومَصْنَعْ
بالمُخْتَصَرْ لِمْقَطَّعْ

جوا المخ عِدّ كَمْ بركان
مْخَبّيهُم عن عين سجّان
ماسك حالي فألف حزام

مِتْعَوِّد عالحَشْرَة من الاجتياح

ضَرَبات لحِّق، هذا جزء من الجزء

لا تقتصر إدارة شعوب بأكملها وكأنّهم أسرى على مفهوم الحبس فقط؛ بل تمتدّ إلى ممارسة السيطرة النفسيّة العميقة. يصف وليد دقّة في صلب أطروحته هذه الجغرافيا السادسة بأداة تُعيد صهر الوعي الفلسطينيّ. تستهدف "السجون الصغيرة" الفلسطينيّين المقاومين، وتسعى ليس فقط إلى اعتقال وعزل من يُعتبرون "تهديدًا أمنيًا"، بل إلى إضعاف إرادتهم أيضًا... إنّها عمليّة إعادة برمجة معرفيّة تهدف إلى قمع المقاومة بشكل جذريّ، وإعادة تشكيل رؤية الفلسطينيّين لنضالهم، خاصّة أولئك الأكثر صمودًا وتمسّكًا بالمبادئ[١٩]. يعتمد المشروع الصهيونيّ على صهر وإذابة الوعي الفلسطينيّ وإعادة تشكيله بقطع الارتباط مع الأرض. يفرض هذا المشروع إحساسًا محدودًا بالانتماء من خلال فصلنا الماديّ الفعليّ عن بعضنا بعضًا، إذ لم تعد الأرض أرضنا ونحن أهلها، بل أصبحنا سكّانًا محاصرين في مناطق محدودة. يُعاد تصنيف الفلسطينيّين من "أصحاب الأرض" ليصبحوا "الحاضرين الغائبين" و"سكّان الأراضي المحتلّة"؛ من معانٍ تكرّم أرواح وأجساد الفلسطينيّين، إلى صورة شديدة الغموض، لا تلعب حتّى دورها القانونيّ. إنّ انسلاخ التصنيفات عن الأرض يمثّل نفيًا وجوديًّا، عبّرت عنه سامرة إسمير بأنّه "تحويل الفلسطينيّين إلى قصبات فارغة، وإجلاء أرواحهم[٢٠]". حالما يُقطع ارتباطنا بالأرض، يُقطع معه انتماؤنا كشعب. ولا نعني بهذا رثاءً لفردوس مفقود، بل نقصد به تكوينًا ماديًّا وجوديًّا يمتد عبر الزمن، الذي بات منفصلًا عن مساره الطبيعيّ، فبدلًا من العيش وفقًا للإيقاع البيئيّ للأرض، حيث يُقاس الزمن بالمواسم والمحاصيل، تُملَى على الحياة الفلسطينيّة حلقات زمنيّة استعماريّة قمعيّة. في هذا الإطار الزمنيّ، تتحوّل الدورات الطبيعيّة إلى مقاييس ربع سنويّة للإنتاجيّة، ويرتبط الحصاد بالربح بدلًا من الاكتفاء الذاتيّ، وتُختَزل الحياة الأصيلة إلى قيمتها التبادليّة. بالرغم من أنّ الكيان الصهيونيّ صُمِّم لنفي وجودنا، يواصل الفلسطينيّون المقاومة بالكفاح المسلّح، والانتفاضات الشعبيّة، والممارسات اليوميّة، ارتباطًا بالأرض ودفاعًا عنها.

١٦
تظهر هذه المصطلحات عدّة مرات في صهر الوعي. انظر، على سبيل المثال، الصفحات ٦١ و٧٥ و٧٦.

١٧
لمزيد من المعلومات حول فكرة وممارسة الترحيل الصهيونيّ، يُرجى مراجعة كتاب نور مصالحة "طرد الفلسطينيّين: مفهوم 'الترانسفير' في الفكر والتخطيط الصهيونيّين، ١٨٨٢-١٩٤٨" (واشنطن العاصمة: مؤسّسة الدراسات الفلسطينيّة، ١٩٩٢).

١٨
مقاطعة، آخر كلمة، حيوان ناطق، ٢٠١٣.

١٩
دقّة، صهر الوعي، ص٣٠.

٢٠
إسمير، ص٦.

غُلّ مِيْت سِنِة

الغضب هذا إلي

هُوْن هو رِبِي

صيف وشِتِي

انْبَسَط وشِقِي

انْهَدّ لَحَدّ ما هِدِي

الضِّفّة محَوّطة مِن جُوّا

جُندي فبُرْج، مِثل جِدِي

يتجلّى تحويل الأرض إلى إقليم ثمّ إلى سجن بشكل أكثر وضوحًا في الإجراءات الاستعماريّة المتعلّقة بالعمل. النظام الإقطاعيّ والقنانة والعبوديّة والامتهان والعمل بالسخرة، وكلّ الأشكال الأخرى للعمل القسريّ الّتي تتمحور حول الزراعة المربحة بالأرض، تظهر وكأنّها تدابير أخلاقيّة انضباطيّة تتناسب مع رأس المال الاستعماريّ. وعليه، يتمّ تشخيص المستعمَرين/ المأسورين/ المستعبَدين على أنّهم يعانون مرضًا أخلاقيًا مزمنًا يعالَج من خلال نظام العمل "التصحيحيّ"، إذ يُعْزَلون جميعًا في مساحات زراعيّة محدودة، والّتي تعمل كتقنيّات مراقبة[٢١] -مثل المزارع والإقطاعيّات والعقارات، وفي السياق الفلسطينيّ مثل البيّارة- الّتي تهدف إلى إنتاج رعايا مجتهدين يلتزمون بمتطلّبات المستعمرة ومراكزها الكبرى.

شو هالعَملة؟ شو هالعُملة؟

شو العَمَل؟ أَغْرَب أَبْعَد

أَبْرَد أَعْقَد بَتْذَكّر كِتْفَك

في الوقت الذي اعتمدت فيه الصهيونيّة على مصادرة الأراضي الزراعيّة الفلسطينيّة لإقامة المستوطنات الاستعماريّة، انتقل العمل الفلسطينيّ إلى القطاعات الصناعيّة، وخاصّة قطاع البناء[٢٢]. أدّت الهيمنة الاستعماريّة الخانقة على الصناعة والتنقّل والتجارة إلى تقييد وتدهور الاقتصاد الفلسطينيّ[٢٣]، ممّا تسبّب بارتفاع معدّلات البطالة وزيادة فائض القوى العاملة، وبذلك، أصبح رجال الطبقة العاملة الفلسطينيّون رهائن اقتصاديّين عند مستعمِريهم، والّذين يتحكّمون بمفهوم إتاحة العمل من خلال نظام تصاريح مدفوعة يتطلّب جمع البيانات البيومتريّة وتتبّع الهواتف المحمولة[٢٤]. في صورة استعماريّة أقلّ ما توصف بالقاسية، يجد الفلسطينيّون أنفسهم يبنون المستوطنات على الأراضي الّتي سُلِبت منهم وهُجِّروا منها.

كيف زعلان وانت اللي تركها؟ بالنّبي ياه...
كيف زعلان عالجدار واحنا اللي بنيناه؟
سامِع الشَّر؟

في ناس ماسكة البلد أمنيًّا
حاطة ناس ماسكة البلد أمنيًّا

ضفّة البنوك والشركات
خُد يا حرامي يا سراق

٢١
Krista Thompson, "The Evidence of Things Not Photographed: Slavery and Historical Memory in the British West Indies," *Representations* 113, no. 1 (2011): 39–71.

٢٢
لدراسة المسار التاريخيّ حول مصادرة الأراضي الفلسطينيّة لصالح الاستيطان الصهيونيّ، يمكنكم مراجعة مقال تشارلز أندرسون، "الانتداب البريطانيّ وأزمة فقدان الأراضي الفلسطينيّة، ١٩٢٩-١٩٣٦" ["The British Mandate and the Crisis of Palestinian Landlessness, ١٩٢٩-١٩٣٦"]، في مجلّة دراسات الشرق الأوسط، العدد ٥٤، رقم ٢ (٢٠١٨)، الصفحات ١٧١-٢١٥. وللمزيد حول العمالة الفلسطينيّة تحت وطأة الصهيونيّة، يرجى الاطّلاع على مقال أندرياس هاكل "العمل المحتلّ: المصادرة من خلال دمج العمّال الفلسطينيّين في إسرائيل" ["Occupied Labour: Dispossession Through Incorporation Among Palestinian Workers in Israel"]، في مجلّة دراسات الاستعمار الاستيطانيّ، العدد ١٣، رقم ١ (٢٠٢٣): الصفحات ٩٦-١١٤.

٢٣
سارة روي، قطاع غزّة: السياسة الاقتصاديّة للإفقار التنمويّ (واشنطن: مؤسّسة الدراسات الفلسطينيّة)، ٢٠١٦.

٢٤
في الوقت نفسه، منح الجهاز الصهيونيّ بالتعاون مع السلطة الفلسطينيّة، نخبة من أصحاب الأعمال امتيازات من خلال إصدار تصريح خاصّ يعرف بـ"بطاقة رجل الأعمال" (BMC). يتيح هذا التصريح لنخبة مختارة من الفلسطينيّين القدرة على التنقّل بحرّيّة نسبيّة عبر الأراضي المحتلّة. تُصْدَر هذه البطاقة من قبل السلطات الاستعماريّة بعد إجراء تقييمات "أمنيّة" صارمة، ويجسّد نظام BMC التفاوت الاقتصاديّ والطبقيّ تحت وطأة الاستعمار. تمنح هذه البطاقة لرجال الأعمال من النخبة، ومعظهم من الضفّة الغربيّة، حرّيّة في الحركة، وتتيح لهم الوصول والتجوّل في فلسطين التاريخيّة لأغراض تجاريّة. تمثّل فئة حاملي هذه البطاقة تواطؤًا يؤسّس ترتيبًا مشتركًا مفيدًا للطرفين: المستعمِر والمستفيد المحلّيّ (الكومبرادور). مدفوعين بالربح والارتهان، ينظر هؤلاء النخبويّون إلى أبناء جلدتهم الفلسطينيّين لا كجماعة واحدة، بل كمستهلكين تحت سلطة استعماريّة لا تتزعزع".

يندرج هذا النظام الاستغلاليّ الفاسد تحت مظلّة الاستعمار الاستيطانيّ الأشمل وممارساته، والّذي بدوره يتأرجح بين إدارة الحياة (السياسات الحيويّة) وإدارة الموت (السياسات النكروويّة). في إطار سعيها إلى الحفاظ على أغلبيّة يهوديّة، ترى الصهيونيّة أنّ "المشكلة الديموغرافيّة" تكمن في الفلسطينيّين، إذ يمثّل وجودنا عقبة مستمرّة وتكاثريّة يجب ضبطها والقضاء عليها إن أمكن، هكذا تُستَنزَف قيمة السكّان الأصليّين، وعبّر فرانز فانون عن ذلك حين أشار إلى وصف المستعمِر للسّكّان الأصليّين بأنّ "القيم لا وجود لها عندهم، بل إنّهم إنكار للقيم[٢٥]"، إذ تُعتَبر أيّ قيمة متبقّية منه غير كامنة وإنّما اقتصاديّة، ممّا يختزل الفلسطينيّين في هذه الحالة، ويحوّلهم إلى وحدات إنتاج واستهلاك تحكمها معدّلات وأسعار السوق. بالتالي، تُسلَب اليد العاملة الفلسطينيّة، وتُصَنّف بعدم المهارة، ولكنّ "القيمة السلبيّة" المستخرجة منها، تحقّق فائضًا للنظام الاستعماريّ، الّذي يستمرّ في تعزيز انقسامنا. إلى أن يحقّق النظام الصهيونيّ أعلى سياسات الموت، ويُنهي الوجود الفلسطينيّ بشكل تامّ، يُنفّذ برنامجًا سياسيًّا-حيويًّا مربحًا، يعمل على إدارتنا جميعًا، لا كشعب، بل كمجموعة من المستهلكين المغتربين، ومخزون من اليد العاملة الخاضعة للمراقبة. وبهذه الطريقة، تتحوّل "الأزمة الديموغرافيّة" إلى مشروع ربحيّ تستفيد منه الصهيونيّة.

قَدَّم. استنّى. خُد. أخَد. انبَسَط.
صِحي. راكض. وقَّف. استنّى.
رِكب. نِزِل. رِكِب. نِزِل. صَفّ.
استَنّى. استَنّى. فوت. فات.
يالله. شافْ. رَدّ. حَسّ. مَحى.
خَلَّص. خُد. أَخَد. اطلَع. طِلِع.
ارْجَع. تِرجَعِش. ارْجَع. اتّاخَدْ.
استَنّى. شاف. طِلِع. حَسّ.

هذه مجرّد حالة واحدة من النفي الأنطولوجيّ/الوجوديّ للفلسطينيّين، إذ يُحَوّلون إلى "جيش احتياطيّ صناعيّ" بلا روح وفقًا للمفهوم الماركسي، حيث يُمارسون عملهم بمعزل وفصل تامّ عن أرضهم. تُعَزِّز استراتيجيّات العمل التي يفرضها الاستعمار الاستيطانيّ نظريّة ماركس حول الاغتراب، ففي هذه الحالة، لا يغترب الفلسطينيّون عن عملهم الّذي لا يستطيعون امتلاك وسائله أو منتجاته فقط، بل يُجْبَرون أيضًا على إنتاج آليّات اغترابهم عن أرضهم[٢٦]. يُفْرَض على الفلسطينيّين تلبية جشع المستعمِر، بدلًا من الانخراط في عمل يحقّق ذات الإنسان ويلبّي احتياجات الشعب ومأواه. عوضًا عن أن يكون عمل يعزّز تحقيق الذات، يتحوّل لفعل إنكار[٢٧]، ويصل حدّ الاغتراب إلى درجة أن تصبح ممارسة العمل نفسه تُبْعِد الفلسطينيّين عن الأرض وتنكر وجودهم. يظلّ هذا الوعي المنكوب عالقًا في الجسد الفلسطينيّ، وكما أشار وليد دقّة، تعمل الصهيونيّة دائمًا على صهره وإعادة تشكيله، لتفرّغ ذاكرة النكبة وتحوّلنا إلى "قصبات فارغة" كما أشارت سامرة إسمير. نُعيد استحضار ذاكرة النكبة نفسيًّا وجسديًّا مع كلّ فعل من أفعال الهدم لمنازلنا وبناء مستوطنات المستعمرين. كلّ طوبة بيضاء تُرَصّ، وكلّ قرميدة حمراء تُنصب، وواجهة حجريّة تُقام، تعيد قصّةسلب أراضي الفلسطينيّين وتهجيرهم، وستبقى منقوشة في ذاكرتنا.

تشويه عن طريق التدمير تشويه عن طريق البنى
بس لسا مقروء.
هدّوا بيته وبيت عَزاه وأخطر اشي ينسمحلنا فيه
هو الهدوء.

٢٥
فرانز فانون، معذّبو الأرض، ترجمة سامي الدروبي وجمال الأتاسي (القاهرة: مدارات للأبحاث والنشر، ٢٠١٤)، ٤١.

٢٦
كارل ماركس، "العمل المغترب"، في المخطوطات الاقتصاديّة والفلسفيّة لعام ١٨٤٤ ترجمة مارتن ميليغان (نيويورك: مطبوعات دوفر، ٢٠٠٧)، الصفحات ٦٧-٨٣.
انظروا أيضًا:
Adam HajYahia, "The Principle of Return: The Repressed Ruptures of Zionist Time," *Parapraxis* (2024), https://www.parapraxismagazine.com/articles/the-principle-of-return.

٢٧
ماركس، ٧٤.

يقول عزمي بشارة: "في القدس وحدها يبدو الحجر الّذي استُخرِج ودُقّ من صخر الجبال غريبًا عن الجبال ذاتها[٢٨]"، إذ تظلّ العمارة الاستيطانيّة مصطنعة وفاقدة لمقوّمات الروح، حتّى عند استيلائها على الموادّ المحلّيّة. تُخفي قشرة الحجر الجيريّ المنهوب وراءها كلّ الهياكل الرخيصة الّتي يُنتجها المستوطنون بزخم كبير. يتكرّر تغليف هذه القشرة في مستوطنات الضفّة الغربيّة في محاولة تزييف ارتباط معماريّ بينها وبين القدس ذات الحدود دائمة التوسّع[٢٩]. كما يغترب الفلسطينيّ عن أرضه وعمله، فإنّ حجر القدس نفسه مغترب أيضًا، إذ يعيش معزولًا عن وظيفته الهيكليّة للبناء، ويبقى قشرةً تغلّف كلّ هذا العنف.

"بِدنا ايّاه زيّه، بس مش زيّه بالزّبط
حامِض حِلو
شوي من هون، شوي من هون
لمسة فَلحة ورَشّة بِدو
فِش داعي للقلق
ولا حدا يروح يِتْلَصَّص
بنجيبهم هُمّ يسّووا
وشوف كيف الهَوا بِتْقَصقَص
مش بس بِدنا ايّاهم ينسوا
بِدنا الذِّكرى يطير معناها
انجنّ الرّوبوت قال في روح
صلحوه، ولو رَفَض، كِبّوا العاهة"
بِعّ عينُه

استحوذ الصهاينة على العمارة التقليديّة الفلسطينيّة، وادّعوا أنّها جزء من تراثهم، ومن جهة أخرى، نظروا إليها بازدراء وتعالٍ، وحاولوا تعريف مبانيهم على أنّها نقيضها المعماريّ التامّ[٣٠]. إنّ هذه الإسقاطات ليست متعارضة، وإنّما تنبع من وعي استعماريّ متناقض، يصوّر العمارة الأصلانيّة على أنّها جميلة وبدائيّة في الوقت نفسه، أو ربّما جميلة لأنّها بدائيّة[٣١]. ارتكازًا على نهج أوروبّيّ حداثيّ للمنطق، صُمِّمت المستوطنات الأولى في تناقض صريح مع منازلنا القرويّة "غير العقلانيّة وغير المنظّمة[٣٢]"، وتؤكّد رؤية ثيودور هرتزل الاستعماريّة: "معقل الحضارة في مواجهة الهمجيّة[٣٣]".

٢٨
عزمي بشارة، الحاجز: شظايا رواية (بيروت: المركز الثقافيّ العربيّ، ٢٠٠٦)، ١٦. انظروا أيضًا كتاب إيال وايزمان، الأرض المجوّفة: الهندسة المعماريّة للاحتلال الإسرائيليّ (لندن: دار فيرسو، ٢٠٠٧)، ٣٣.

٢٩
إنّ الأصالة المصطنعة للصهيونيّة ليست جديدة في حدّ ذاتها، إذ ورثت ممارسة الحفاظ على واجهات القدس الحجريّة والترويج لها من مرسوم بريطانيّ صدر عام ١٩١٨. انظروا إلى مقدّمة الحاكم العسكريّ البريطانيّ رونالد ستورز في كتاب "القدس، ١٩٠٨-١٩٢٠"، الصادر عن مجلس جمعيّة دعم القدس [Pro-Jerusalem Society Council]، من تحرير تشارلز روبرت آشبي (لندن: جون موراي، ١٩٢١). وأنابيل وارتون، "إعادة تشكيل القدس" [Jerusalem Remade]، في "الحداثة والشرق الأوسط: العمارة والسياسة في القرن العشرين" [Modernism and the Middle East: Architecture and Politics in the Twentieth Century]، من تحرير ساندي إيسنشتات وكشوار رزفي (سياتل: دار نشر جامعة واشنطن، ٢٠٠٨)، الصفحات ٣٩-٦٠. وفصل ندي أبو سعادة، "لقاءات حضريّة: صناعة صورة المدينة في فلسطين الانتدابيّة" ["Urban Encounters: Imagining the City in Mandate Palestine"] في كتاب "تصوير وتخيّل فلسطين: التصوير الفوتوغرافيّ والحداثة والعدسة التوراتيّة، ١٩١٨- ١٩٤٨"، [Imaging and Imagining Palestine: Photography, Modernity, and the Biblical Lens] من تحرير كارين سانشيز سامر وساري زنانيري (ليدن: بريل، ٢٠٢١)، ٣٧٠-٣٧١.

٣٠
في خطاب ألقاه آرثر روبين، "أبو الاستيطان الصهيونيّ" الألمانيّ، أمام جمعيّة الاستعمار اليهوديّة في فيينا عام ١٩٠٨، صرّح بأنّه "على عكس القرى العربيّة البائسة الّتي تتكوّن من أكواخ الطين المحروق، تبدو المستعمرات اليهوديّة، بشوارعها الواسعة وبيوتها الحجريّة القويّة وأسقفها المكسوّة بالقرميد الأحمر، كواحات فعليّة من الثقافة". آرثر روبين، ثلاثة عقود في فلسطين (القدس: شوكن، ١٩٣٦)، ٩؛ وارتون، "إعادة تشكيل القدس"، ٤٥.

٣١
اعترف توماس ليترسدورف، مهندس مستوطنة معاليه أدوميم (أراضي بلدتي العيزريّة وأبو ديس)، قائلًا: "إنّي أنظر إلى شكل القرى العربيّة بعين الحسد. يكمن جمال القرية العربيّة في طبيعتها التراكميّة وغير المنطقيّة [irrational] إلى حدّ ما". إران تمي-تاويل، "لتبني المدينة من الصفر: مقابلة مع المهندس المعماريّ توماس م. ليترسدورف"، في احتلال مدنيّ: سياسات العمارة الإسرائيليّة، من تحرير رافي سيغال وإيال وايزمان (تل أبيب ولندن: بابل ودار فيرسو، ٢٠٠٣)، ١٦٠؛ مذكور في وايزمان، أرض جوفاء [Hollow Land]، ٤٤.

٣٢
وايزمان، ٤٤.

٣٣
ثيودور هرتزل، دولة اليهود: محاولة لإيجاد حلّ حديث للمسألة اليهوديّة [A Jewish State: An Attempt at a Modern Solution of the Jewish Question]، ترجمة سيلفي دافيدغور (نيويورك: شركة ماكابيان للنشر، ١٩٠٤)، ٢٩. يعزّز الطراز المعماريّ الحديث للمستوطنات الصهيونيّة أسلوب "المدينة المسيّجة"، وكأنّها مدينة حدائقيّة -وفقًا لنظرية وأسلوب تخطيط المهندس المعماري البريطاني إبنيزر هوارد- تُعطي شعورًا بالألفة لدى المستوطنين الأوروبّيّين الّذين دُعُوا إلى أرض غريبة. (وهذا مشابه لنظام الغابات المكونة من أشجار الصنوبر الغازية والقابلة للاشتعال الّتي زرعها الصندوق القوميّ اليهوديّ على بقايا أراضي القرى الفلسطينيّة المدمّرة، لإخفاء آثارنا وخلق استمراريّة زائفة مع المناظر الطبيعيّة الأوروبّيّة). لمزيد من المعلومات حول هذا المشروع، يمكن الرجوع إلى مقال أريج الأشهب ومارتا وودز، "Between the Pines: More-than-human Narratives beyond the Jewish National Fund Forests"، في كتيّب *Researching Palestine*، تحرير آلاء عبد، كريس هاردينغ، وماريا خوري (دار جاسر، ٢٠٢٤): ٤٧-٥٥.

ومع ذلك، يبقى المستعمِر غريبًا عن الأرض بشكل فجّ، رغم كلّ محاولاته القسريّة لترسيخ نفسه وتجذيرها في الأرض، ولكنّ بيئته المستورَدة غير قادرة أبدًا على خلق انسجام بيئيّ طبيعيّ، إذ تظلّ كما وصفها إدوارد سعيد، "قوّة تدخّليّة وقحة"، تنتشر وتلتهم أراضينا مثل "سرطان متفشٍّ[٣٤]".

مستعمرة جمبُه لبيتي مبسوطة
عحالها من بعيد بتغاوز

بتضلها تكبر سرطان عالجبل
نفسها تنزل تطردنا أنا عارف

تمثّل الجهود الاستعماريّة في إخفاء حقيقة السلب والتهجير محاولة لمنع العودة الحتميّة، ومحو ذاكرة الأرض، وبدون الأرض لن يكون ثمّة كيان نقاومه أو شيء نستعيده. يجادل جوزيف مسعد أنّ رفض الفلسطينيّين الاستسلام وقبول موت فلسطين (وبالتّالي عدم إمكانيّة استعادتها)، مشخّص استعماريًّا كمرض[٣٥]، إذ صنّفت الصهيونيّة ارتباط الفلسطينيّين بأرضهم وعدم رغبتهم في نسيانها أو التخلّي عنها كاضطراب نفسيّ تسمّيه معاداة الساميّة[٣٦]، والّذي لا يمكن علاجه إلّا من خلال استئصال "العقل المريض" الفلسطينيّ (صهر وعيه) أو تصفية الجماهير المقاومة (إبادة شاملة). يمكننا اعتبار نظام استغلال العمالة الصهيونيّ أحد "العلاجات" الّتي تُفرض على نطاق واسع لمواجهة توق الفلسطينيّين إلى الوطن. يظنّ المستعمر أنّه عندما يمحو ويطمس أيّ أثر ويقتل إمكانيّة وجود الوطن، فإنّه بذلك يؤكّد عدم وجوده، وأنّه لم يكن هناك واحدًا من الأساس لنتوق إليه. يعزّز البناء والتعمير الدائم والمتكرّر للمستعمرات على أرضنا فكرة فقدان الوطن، إذ يرسّخ الوجود الاستيطانيّ، ويعيد إنتاج اغترابنا. كما يُجبَر الفلسطينيّون على المشاركة في بناء زنازينهم الخاصّة، من الحجارة إلى الجدران، في دائرة مفرغة من التعذيب تحوّل الأرض الّتي أحبّوها يومًا إلى سجن. روتين مميت يجبر العمّال على الاستيقاظ في الساعة الرابعة صباحًا والانتقال من فورد إلى فورد[٣٧] ومن نقطة تفتيش إلى أخرى. نستطيع أن نحسب ساعات الإذلال، إذ يمكن أن تمتدّ من ساعة واحدة أو ثلاث لتصل حتّى تسع ساعات، وذلك حسب مزاج المستعمِر، وهنا يُجَسَّد هذا الاغتراب في الحرص على الوصول إلى العمل باكرًا للمشاركة في بناء المستعمرة. إنّه عمل ينكر الأرض والذات، ويبعدنا مرارًا وتكرارًا عن الـ"هنا" الّتي نعيش فيها، ليجعلنا غرباء وكأنّنا لم "نكن" يومًا: لم نكن موجودين، لم نُنف أو نُسلب، فقط لم نكن هنا ولا جزءًا من هذه الأرض.

كيلوَك ٣ دقايق
كيلُوي ٣ ساعات

٣٤
إدوارد سعيد، بعد السماء الأخيرة: حيوات فلسطينيّة [*After the Last Sky: Palestinian Lives*]، (نيويورك: كتب بانتثون، ١٩٨٦)، ٧٢.

٣٥
مسعد، "العمل الثقافيّ لاستعادة فلسطين"، ٢٠١٥.

٣٦
مسعد، ١٨٨: "الفلسطينيّون، رغم حزنهم على فقدان موتاهم وطريقة حياتهم، وتهجيرهم من منازلهم وأراضيهم، وفقدان استقلالهم لصالح السيطرة الإسرائيليّة، ما زالوا يقاومون الحداد على فكرة فقدان فلسطين منذ عام ١٩٤٨ كفقدان نهائيّ، بل يستمرّون في استحضار ارتباطهم بها والتخطيط لاستعادتها. هذا الإصرار يُعْتَبَر من قِبَل أعداء الفلسطينيّين بأنّه مرضيّ، وغالبًا ما يُحَدّد بأنّه 'معادٍ للساميّة'، وهو في حدّ ذاته مرض يُشَخَّص نفسيًّا. من منظور التحليل النفسيّ، يتّهم الصهاينة الفلسطينيّين بالمعاداة للساميّة المزعومة كنوع من سرد فشل الفلسطينيّين المفترض في الحداد".

٣٧
الفوردات هي حافلات صغيرة تتّسع لسبعة ركّاب، وتُستخدم كوسيلة للنقل العامّ في الضفّة الغربيّة. يُسْتَخدم هذا الإسم بشكل عامّ للإشارة إلى جميع هذه الحافلات، بغضّ النظر عن الشركة المصنّعة الفعليّة لها.

٤

كان برتاح لونهم أشباح
ما بخّوفنيش صدى الرياح
ما بتخوّفنيش العتمة بتاتًا
انا لمخّوفني معيش سلاح

المعظم عدوّ

٣٨
في قراءة التاريخ الاستعماريّ بشكل مقارن، أشار مسعد إلى حدث المهرجان الموسيقي الإسرائيليّ الّذي أقيم بالقرب من غزّة المحاصرة أنّه "ليس وضعًا مقصورًا على الإسرائيليين، فقد صرّح المدعي العام الجنوب أفريقي في مستعمرة ناميبيا الاستيطانية التي كانت تحتلها جنوب أفريقيا في عام ١٩٨٣، أنّ 'المجتمع الأبيض ليس لديه أدنى فكرة عما يحدث في منطقة العمليات'، حيث كانت مقاومة السود على أشدها. وأضاف أنّ 'البيض في جنوب البلاد يواصلون إقامة الحفلات'. وقد أوضح مؤرخو النضال النامبي أنه 'لا غرابة في أن البيض نتيجة تعودهم على غضّ الطّرف عن المقاومة المحتدّة في ضواحي السود التي لا تبعد أكثر من خمسة أميال عن منازلهم، قد تجاهلوا الحرب القائمة بالقرب منهم'". جوزيف مسعد، "كيف تقوم إسرائيل والغرب بتشويه سمعة الفلسطينيّين باعتبارهم معادين للساميّة"، عرب ٢١، ١٨ تشرين الثاني/ نوفمبر ٢٠٢٣.

٣٩
بيت من قصيدة "يا ظلام السجن خيّم" للصحفيّ السوريّ المناضل نجيب الريس، الّتي "وردت على لسان الشهيد محمّد خليل أبو جمجوم، عندما أبلغه مدير سجن عكّا البريطانيّ، هو ورفيقاه عطا الزير وفؤاد حجازي بقرار الإعدام، فشرعوا في ترديد النشيد يا ظلام السجن خيّم، ونُفِّذ حكم الإعدام فيهم صباح الثلاثاء١٩٣٠/٦/١٧". أسامة الأشقر، "يا ظلام السجن خيّم"، حكاية مع نشيد خالد!" الجزيرة، ٢٠١٧. https://www.aljazeera.net/blogs/-/٢٠١٧/١٠/١٨/يا-ظلام-السجن-خيم-حكاية-مع-نشيد-خالد.

٤٠
كتاب باتريك وولف، الاستعمار الاستيطانيّ وتحوّل الأنثروبولوجيا: السياسة والشعريّة لحدث إثنوغرافيّ [Settler Colonialism and the Transformation of Anthropology: The Politics and Poetics of an Ethnographic Event] (نيويورك: كونتينوم، ١٩٩٨)؛ ومقاله "الاستعمار الاستيطانيّ وإبادة السكّان الأصليّين" [Settler Colonialism and the Elimination of the Native] في مجلّة الأبحاث حول الإبادة [*Journal of Genocide Research*]، العدد ٨، رقم ٤ (٢٠٠٦): ٣٨٧-٤٠٩. انظروا أيضًا لورينزو فيراشيني، "دفاعًا عن دراسات الاستعمار الاستيطانيّ" ["Defending Settler Colonial Studies"] في مجلّة الدراسات التاريخيّة الأستراليّة، العدد ٤٥ رقم ٣ (٢٠١٤): ٣٣١-١٦. وللاطّلاع على نظريّة النكبة المستمرّة، انظروا الى كتاب الراحل إلياس خوري النكبة المستمرّة (بيروت: دار الآداب، ٢٠٢٣).

إنّ نفي الصهيونيّة للذات الفلسطينيّة، عبر القول "إنّنا لسنا موجودين، ولم نكن يومًا كذلك"، لا يشكّل فقط قمعًا وإنكارًا لهويّتنا كشعب، ولكنّه أيضًا يُعْتَبر الستار الّذي يخفي المستعمِر تحته الحقيقة المكبوتة، وهي تهديد فكرة العودة الحتميّة للفلسطينيّين إلى أراضيهم. صورة عودتنا مدفونة في أعماق العقل الصهيونيّ إلى درجة تمكّنهم من تنظيم مهرجان موسيقى ترانس من أجل "السلام"، والذي يُقام بجوار شعب محاصر لأكثر من سبعة عشر عامًا دون أيّ شعور بالتناقض[٣٨]، والحبس والدفن للسكّان الأصليّين وحده هو ما يضمن للمستوطنين الحفاظ على أوهامهم وبقائهم في حالة من التنويم الاستعماريّ. فيظلّ حصار غزّة والمعاناة الناتجة عنه حاضرَيْن في وعي المستوطنين، إذ يتمّ فرضهم بشكل فعّال وواضح في السياسات الصهيونيّة، وفي الرأي العامّ. وفي الواقع، إنّ الموت والذلّ الناتجين عن الحصار ليسا مهمَلَين أبدًا، بل يتمّ تغطيتهما وإحصاؤهما وتوثيقهما بشكل مستمرّ. وبينما يتكرّر نعت غزّة بـ "السجن المفتوح" يوميًّا من قِبَل عدد مهول من السياسيّين حول العالم واللجان الّتي لا تتوقّف عن جمع الأدلّة، وجلسات المحاكمة الدوليّة الّتي تعقد وتؤجّل، يظلّ السؤال: لمن تُكْتَب كلّ تقارير حقوق الإنسان هذه؟ وهل تبقى أيّ من الإحصاءات الأخرى الّتي غفلنا عن عدّها؟ تتراءى خلف كلّ هذه الضجّة والتساؤلات حقيقة واحدة، وهي حتميّة العودة، حتّى عندما تكون حبيسة طبقات من الحكم الاستعماريّ والنيوليبراليّ.

لا حامي حالي ولا الحَوَلِي في هاي اللحظة، عم بَمُرّ بموقف
أصعب من كلشي شفته، الصراحة بدي مساعدة
كل جانب من عيشتي ضاوي طوارئ عندي في زعل هين
يا دوب أنا عايش بس راضي هسّا و باللي جاي بعدين
لسّا بنحكي عن صاحب الأرض هندي، بالله عليك

يـا ظلامَ الـقبرِ خيّمْ   إنّنا نــهوى الظلاما
لـيسَ بعدَ الموتِ إلّا   فجرُ مجدٍ يتسامى [٣٩]

تشهد النكبة على أنّ الاستعمار بنية ممنهجة، وليس حدثًا معزولًا[٤٠]، ولكنّ ذلك يحمل في طيّاته خطر تأكيد أبديّته خطابيًّا، إذ يوحي مفهوم البنية الممنهجة بالدوام والثبات واستحالة التغيير. من المؤكّد أنّ النكبة مستمرّة على المستوى الهيكليّ، ولكنّها أيضًا بالمقابل مربوطة باستمراريّة مقاومة الحالة الكارثيّة الّتي تنتج عنها، حتّى ينتهي دَوْمُها. يعكس دافع المستعمِر لأرشفة النكبة رغبتَه في التغاضي عنها ككارثة وتجاوزها ليتمكّن من المضيّ قدمًا، ويقوم بذلك من خلال تجميد الفلسطينيّين في زمن

"الماضي المنتهي"، وبهذا الزمن، تحاول الصهيونيّة دفن صورتنا المفعمة بحتميّة العودة. يصنع المستعمِر وهم التقدّم فوق الأنقاض، باستمراريّة مزيّفة تتمثّل بواجهة حجريّة هشّة وجوفاء، تحجب أنقاض القرية الفلسطينيّة المقموعة، والّتي تنتظر بفارغ الصبر أن تعود إلى الحياة[٤١]. لا يُنْتِج المستعمِر التاريخ (لأنّه ليس لديه ماض متجذّر يبني عليه) بل يقمعه، يمتلك فقط سرديّة الدمار المبنيّة على التشويه، ويوهم نفسه بالانتماء، بينما يدفن خوفه الدائم من عودة السكّان الأصليّين.

نعامة ترفصك
بيلبس ثوب فلسطيني وبِذْبِك يعني بِرُقْصَك[٤٢].

كم واحد منهم غيّر اسمه لمّا دخل
حواكير، شوارع فيها أصوات تاريخ ودم
بتعرف إنه السلام أجدد وإنّه الحرب أقدم؟

على نقيض المُستعمِر، تُحَرِّك الجماهير المقاومة عجلة التاريخ، وينتج عن استمرار تلك المقاومة وعدم اكتمال النكبة قمع الوجود الفلسطينيّ في العقليّة الصهيونيّة. يذكّرنا المفكّر الفلسطينيّ خالد عودة الله، "لم تكن النكبة في وقائعها الميدانيّة نكبة خالصة، فقد تضمّنت وقائعها مقاومة وقتالًا حتّى الطلقة الأخيرة، وهي ذات 'جدوى مستمرّة' إلى يومنا هذا[٤٣]". عندما نتحدّث عن نكبة الفلسطينيّين المستمرّة، فإنّنا نتناول كلًّا من الحالة الفلسطينيّة المنكوبة والجهد المستمرّ لمقاومتها. تُوطّد المقاومة علاقتنا بالأرض، وترتكز في صلبها على قناعة العودة؛ وتؤكّد وجودنا لا في الوعي المصهور وأرواحه المسلوبة، بل كشعب عنيد يناضل دائمًا من أجل التحرير.

قَدْ ما طاخ الطيخ ما بهمّش
بدوّخ رصاصة
فِش تصيبيني يا مَكّارة
وين أنا، ما بتعرفيش أي حارة
بلّشتي تْخَبْصي واتدعسي عاللّاصة

٤١
باسل عبّاس وروان أبو رحمة، رغم ذلك، قناعي منيع، ٢٠١٦.

٤٢
مقاطعة، ٢٠١٣.

٤٣
خالد عودة الله، "خالد عودة الله: فلسطين من القدس إلى غزّة"، في مقابلة أجراها عبد الرحيم الشيخ، مؤسّسة الدراسات الفلسطينيّة، العدد ١٣٧ (٢٠٢٤): ٧٠.

يصف المثقّف المشتبك الشهيد باسل الأعرج[٤٤] المقاومة بأنّها جدوى مستمرّة تزدادُ مكاسبها الاجتماعيّة والتاريخيّة باستمرار. كتب الأعرج: "المقاومة جدوى مستمرّة، كلّ ثمن تدفعه في المقاومة إن لم تحصّله في حياتك ستحصل عليه لاحقًا[٤٥]". إنّ الاستثمار في المقاومة هو الإيمان بحتميّة وجود احتمال آخر، إذ يتلاشى الحدّ الفاصل بين الحياة والآخرة، وبين النفس والشهادة. يمنحنا هذا الاستثمار احتمالات متمثّلة في عدّة أشكال للعودة: العودة إلى الأرض والذات، والعودة إلى الكلّ الجمعيّ، وعودة القيمة الاجتماعيّة والثقافيّة، وعودة الفلسطينيّ المقموع في ثنايا عقل المستعمِر. في جولة تاريخيّة حول منطقة جنين، شرح الأعرج المسار التاريخيّ لاستثمار جنين في المقاومة، من الاحتلال البريطانيّ والاستيطان الصهيونيّ خلال الثلاثينيّات وصولًا إلى إخلاء الاستعمار الصهيونيّ أربع مستوطنات وهي حومش وكاديم وجانيم وصانور، والّتي تحيط بالمخيّم بعد سبعة عقود في عام ٢٠٠٥[٤٦]. رافق ذلك انسحاب الجيش الإسرائيليّ من غزّة وتحريرها الحاسم في العام نفسه، والّذي تضمّن تفكيك إحدى وعشرين مستوطنة وعشرات من النقاط العسكريّة؛ عمليّة تؤكّد أهمّيّة المقاومة، وأنّ عائد استثمارها هو استعادة ملموسة وعودة إلى الأرض[٤٧].

٤٤
دائمًا يشار إلى باسل الأعرج بـ"المثقّف المشتبك"، بسبب التزامه العميق بالمقاومة السياسيّة. وقد أكّد الأعرج نفسه على أهمّيّة الاشتباك السياسيّ، إذ قال: "بدّك تصير مثقّف، بدّك تصير مشتبك، إذا ما بدك تشتبك...لا منك ولا من ثقافتك". باسل الأعرج، صوتي واضح (بيروت: دار المودّة، ٢٠٢٢)، ١٣.

٤٥
الأعرج، صوتيّ واضح، ٧٤. على عكس "النشاط السياسيّ" المدعوم من المنظّمات غير الحكوميّة، الّذي يعطي الأولويّة للأهداف قصيرة الأمد المتوافقة مع أجندات المانحين ودورات التمويل، فإنّ المقاومة هي نضال مستمرّ يهدف في النهاية إلى التحرير. بعد اتّفاقيّة أوسلو، أُضْفِي الطابع المؤسّسيّ على النشاط الفلسطينيّ بشكل ممنهج، ممّا أدّى إلى تفكّك المجتمع المدنيّ والجهود الشعبيّة الّتي كانت تشكّل تاريخيًّا العمود الفقريّ للمقاومة الشعبيّة. أدّى هذا التحوّل إلى مشاريع تهدف لنتائج فوريّة وقابلة للقياس بدلًا من الهدف البعيد المدى للتحرير. لمزيد من المعلومات عن التحوّل إلى نموذج المنظّمات غير الحكوميّة في فلسطين، انظروا ساري حنفي ولندا طبر، بروز النخبة الفلسطينيّة المعولمة: المانحون، والمنظّمات الدوليّة والمنظّمات غير الحكوميّة المحلّيّة (ميشيغان: جامعة ميشيغان، ٢٠٠٩).

٤٦
الأعرج، "المقاومة وجدواها... نموذج ريف جنين"، ١٩ كانون الأوّل/ ديسمبر ٢٠١٤، دائرة سليمان الحلبي للدراسات الاستعمارية والتحرّر المعرفيّ، فيديو يوتيوب، ٢:٠٤. https://www.youtube.com/watch?list=PLB٨AcJNYK&٠_v=NIoiBnZepTPAQW٠eIGgqSfGhKZXIrsp٢V.

٤٧
فرض الكيان الصهيونيّ حصارًا استعماريًّا كعقوبة جماعيّة على مقاومة غزّة، ممّا يحيل تحقيق هذا الاستثمار بشكل كامل. ورغم ذلك، تواصل غزّة الاستثمار في المقاومة والتحرير، كما رأينا في مسيرات العودة في ٢٠١١ الّتي أُجْهِضَت بشكل مبكّر، لتستأنف في ٢٠١٨ -٢٠١٩ ومرّة أخرى في ٢٠٢٣. هذه ليست سوى لحظات مختارة في استثمار مستمرّ والتزام بالعودة.

يا **** ******

يويا

جيناكم غفلة

يويا

من فوق وتحتا

يويا

سوّينا زحمة

يويا

قلنا بِع عينه

يويا

قلنا يا عيبه

يويا

لأوّل مرة

يويا

اتزَلَّط أبو شقرة

يويا

ميّة وخمسين

يويا

عام في التّكوين

يويا

أعرجنا صادِق

يويا

كل خطوة فادت

اخ يرحم روحك

قال خالد عودة الله: "في ٧ تشرين الأوّل/ أكتوبر ٢٠٢٣، لم تبد النكبة مستمرّة، بل حدثًا تاريخيًّا طارئًا عندما مارس لاجئو قرى قضاء غزّة العودة الفعليّة إلى ديارهم[٤٨]". أطلقت المقاومة سراح النكبة من سيطرة الأرشفة والتنظير الاستعماريّ بهدف إنهائها. لا ينحصر دور المقاومة في تقديم حلول سياسيّة، بل يكمن في ممارسة واجب، وليس الحقّ، في العودة[٤٩]. يمثّل طوفان الأقصى عودة المقموعين المخترِقة لحواجز المستعمِر الماديّة والنّفسيّة الّتي أدّت إلى عقود من الموت والهوان. يمثّل الطوفان شرخًا كبيرًا في المفهوم الصهيونيّ للزمن، إذ عاند الساعة الاستعماريّة وأحدث صدعًا في مجال الزمن الصهيونيّ، حيث يلتقي "الزمن الموازي" للسجن الصغير مع "الزمن الاجتماعيّ" للسجن الكبير[٥٠]. وبذلك، يتوجّب علينا قراءة إصرار المقاومة على تحرير الأسرى الفلسطينيّين كجزء من الحتميّة الكبرى للعودة، للوصول إلى لحظة تلتحم فيها الجغرافيّات الستّ معًا.

قبل حدعشر سنة
صحّلّي أتعرّف عليه
كان لسّا طالع من حبسة حدعشر سنة
قال لي "في تاريخ الشعوب اللي قاومت،
٤٪ منهم بس اللي بقاوموا
احنا النسبة عِنّا كتير أعلى
فاتّطّمّن"
"سأقول ما لا تحتمله حضارة الآخرين..[٥١]"
..حياتنا أثمن من حياة المستعمِرين.

٤٨
عودة الله والشيخ (٢٠٢٤): ٧٠.

٤٩
بشارة، "فلسطين قضيّة العرب أم مشكلة الفلسطينيّين؟ أسئلة النكبة والتاريخ"، ١٨ أيّار ٢٠٠٩ الجامعة الأمريكيّة في بيروت، ١:٤٧:٣١ تمّ بثّه مباشرًا وأرشفته من قبل الجزيرة العربيّة، https://www.youtube.com/watch?v=١WPPAFA٩ZJs.

٥٠
انظروا رسالة دقّة المنشورة في عرب ٤٨، ٣١ أكتوبر ٢٠١٠.
https://www.arab٤٨.com//ثقافة-وفنون/نص/٢٠١٠/١٠/٣١/رسالة-الأسير-وليد-دقة-في-اليوم-الأول-من-عامه-العشرين-في-الأسر!. انظروا أيضًا الشيخ، "المكان الموازي"، خاصة الصفحات ١٩٧-٢٠٠.

٥١
خالد جمعة، "قليل ممّا ستقول غزّة عمّا قليل"، مجلّة الدراسات الفلسطينيّة، العدد ١٣٧ (٢٠٢٤)، ص ٣١٩.

هاي المصطلحات جايبة دَوَرْنا
قد ما فتّشنا ودَوَّرْنا
عالعَمَية الضّو وَزْنا
احنا مش نَفْس الحكاي
بس كَماتْنا بنحسّ في بَرَكةْ
من يوم يومنا نقاوم، فبَرْكِي
اليوم تاريخنا يقتل الفَبْرَكِة
قبل بكرا اللّي جاي
جوّا الزمّن في كَمْشة طلق
عديم إحساس كان يرقص
شاف السما، ركض، انطلق
قلب عربي وحكى عليّ الطلاق
ما بعمري أرجع أطلع من هالولاي
احنا فأقوى مرحلة، فلا تكون سَلْبِيّ
هاي الخرايط خَرْطَت سَلْبِيْ
الفراغ صدى الدم سالْ بِيْهْ
كله مرسوم بعناي

المقاوَمة مِش رومانسيّات
هي ممارسة الرَفْض
ال لا الإيجابية
وطمأنة النّبض

أن تقاوم، يعني ببساطة أن ترفض الانسحاق تحت الثقل البنيويّ للنكبة، ويتجلّى ذلك في إعادة بناء الفلسطينيّين لمنازلهم المدمّرة تحت القصف المستمرّ. يستوقفنا الصمود الفلسطينيّ، وخصوصًا صمود غزّة، ولكن تبقى الإشكاليّة في إضفاء الطابع الرومانسيّ للمقاومة والعودة. ففي الرومانسيّة استسلام للتجريد، لتجريد فلسطين وخاصّة غزّة من كلّ التضحيات الفعليّة الّتي قدّمتها. لا يتمثّل التجريد فقط في لغة المجتمع الدوليّ، بل نراها داخل المجتمع الفلسطينيّ، خاصّة من الطبقة البرجوازيّة الكومبرادوريّة، الّتي تستمرّ في رمي غزّة في الحيّز السالب، مباعدة بين سكّانها، إذ تطلق عليهم الغزّيّين لتفرّقهم عن كونهم من نسيج شعبنا الفلسطينيّ[٥٢]. يعترف هذا الفصل بالحدود الاستعماريّة، ويعزل قطاع غزّة في واقع من القمع والإدانة. من المؤكّد أنّ غزّة لا تقع خارج فلسطين، ولكنّ الحصار الصهيونيّ الخانق ومؤيّديه جعلوها مكانًا بعيدًا ومعزولًا على المستويين الخطابيّ والماديّ. الآن، مع بداية الشهر الثاني عشر من الإبادة -والّذي يتوازى مع إنكار واقع الإبادة عالميًا- نرى نتائج عزل غزّة على المستوى السياسيّ وأثره على التحرير.

شعب صابر بالغصب. صدمة غزة قلب
شعبي في أضعف وأقوى حالاته بنفس الوقت
أمّا المقاومة تضاعفت آخر ١٥٠ سنة فيوم واحد
ولا ظفر راح عالفاضي آخر ١٥٠ سنة ساحت

انتقام الأطفال تعبير طاهِر
دروع الإمّيات ضدّ الخونة طاهِر
كُلّ ما بِنشِدّ، أَضعافُه بِحاصِر
أَضعافُه بِدْبَح، رووس وخواصِر
بِشَتِّتوا الانتفاضة، بِشَتِّتوا المساطر
كابوسهُم رَجْعِتنا. فَبِقَتْلوا مَقابِر
في فرق بين متظاهِر ومتظاهِر
التّاني كَذّاب، والأوّل طاهِر

٥٢
تُعَدّ الغالبيّة العظمى من سكان غزّة أحفاد اللاجئين من المدن والبلدات الساحليّة شمال غزة، الذين هُجِّروا قسريًّا من قِبَل الميلشيات الصهيونيّة عام ١٩٤٨.

نعود في ذاكرتنا إلى قرار المحكمة الاستعماريّة بتهجير العائلات الفلسطينيّة من حيّ الشيخ جرّاح في القدس لصالح المستوطنين في أيّار ٢٠٢١، والانتفاضة الشعبيّة الّتي اشتعلت في كلّ فلسطين. كانت لحظة قصيرة ولكنّها علامة فارقة ومهمّة من التعاضد الاجتماعيّ والوعي السياسيّ العابر للحدود الاستعماريّة، وخاصّة في الداخل المحتلّ الّذي انتفض ضدّ المستعمِر لأوّل مرّة منذ عقود. تدعونا هذه الانتفاضة المتميّزة ضدّ الاستعمار الصهيونيّ الاستيطانيّ، والّتي اشتعلت من قلب القدس إلى الأراضي المحتلّة عام ١٩٤٨، وفي رام اللّه لفترة وجيزة وخاصّة بعد أن اغتالت السلطة الفلسطينيّة الناشط العنيد نزار بنات للتساؤل عن بلوغ ذروتها بقصف غزّة. في إطار مقاومتنا للمصادرة ونزع الملكيّة، كيف لنا أن نرى هتاف: "يا غزّة ياللّه، من شان اللّه" وما يتضمّنه من توقّع تتدخّل فيه غزّة لتسعف القدس، على أنّه أمر مسلّم به؟

أنا الوعي اللي بفلت وقت ما بده
هوية ضفة تستبده
إذا حدا من غزة سمعني بتغنوج،
يا إمّا حيضحك يا إمّا حيكفر

يشاركنا المعارِض السياسيّ المصريّ علاء عبد الفتّاح تساؤلًا من داخل سجن طرة شديد الحراسة في القاهرة في عام ٢٠٢١: "أيحقّ للأسير أن يطلب النصرة من المحاصر؟[٥٣]". في ظلّ التفكير في معنى العيش في السجون الصغيرة والكبيرة، وتجاوز القيود المادّيّة والأيديولوجيّة، وأهمّيّة التضامن والحشد والتنظيم الحقيقيّ على جميع الجبهات، يصبح سؤال علاء عبد الفتّاح أكثر إلحاحًا. يشير خالد عودة اللّه إلى دور غزّة في الدفاع عن القدس وحماية المسجد الأقصى ضدّ الاستعمار، وخلقها لتوازن يهدّد المستعمر باندلاع حرب كبرى. لكنّنا نرى أنّ هناك علاقة اعتماديّة نشأت بين غزّة والقدس، حلّت محلّ التضامن في الوعي الجمعيّ نتيجة لأخذ دور غزّة في التحرير الفلسطينيّ كأمر مسلّم به[٥٤]. لهذه الديناميكيّة الأحاديّة تداعيات مضنية. كيف يمكن لنا أن نعرّف أنفسنا كشعب في ظلّ هذا الاعتماد، والّذي في قلبه يكمن انفصال خطير؟ كيف تشكّلت هذه المعادلة حيث الطرف الذي جرأ واخترق الحدود الاستعمارية يدفع ثمنًا أبهظ بكثير من الطرف الآخر ؟ "وصلنا إلى مرحلة من المراحل اللّي صارت الناس تطلب من غزّة تدخل في حرب ضروس" يعلّق عودة اللّه، "سوف يسقط من غزّة مئات وعشرات من الشهداء من أجل أن توقف مسيرة للمستوطنين[٥٥]". النقد هنا ليس للمقاومة، بل للخطورة الناجمة عن العلاقة الاعتماديّة والتوقّعات الّتي

تشكّلت أيديولوجيًا من بعض شرائح مجتمعنا بشأن دور غزّة كواجهة مقاومة حصريّة لفلسطين. يقلّل توقّع التضحية فداءً للقدس من قيمة حياة شعبنا في غزّة، بما في ذلك مقاتلونا الأحرار وهم في طريقهم للشهادة، والّذين لم نتمكّن من الحداد عليهم بعد. كما أنّ هذا التّوقّع يعجز عن مواجهة التقبّل الاجتماعيّ لواقع الحصار الدائم، علاوة على تطبيع قصف غزّة الّذي استمرّ لعقدين.

بصرخوا عالكاميرا
بنتفرج زي أميرة
بعيدة فقلعة فجزيرة
والواقع بيننا ساعتين
نصنا بده ينبسط
زيح فيديو، هات كلب وقط
نشد بعض قالت الست
كبيرها نحطّها فاغنيتين
شطّحت وبطّحت
يحرّروها مش غلط
من هون لوقتها هات قطط
لا تلومنا يا غراب البين
بس نصنا التاني مرابط
عباب القرية حاطط
عصاية وضو مْشارط
يهجموا الأندال في الليل

٥٣
علاء عبد الفتّاح، "فلسطين ع البال" مدى مصر، ١٦ أيلول ٢٠٢١.

٥٤
خالد عودة الله، "إيش عملت فينا الحرب على غزّة؟... مع الباحث خالد عودة الله"، بودكاست القدس، فيديو يوتيوب، ١:١٩:١٨، ٢٤ أبريل ٢٠٢٤، https://www.youtube.com/watch?v=sfz٠H٥pzZ٠g.

٥٥
خالد عودة الله، "إيش عملت فينا الحرب على غزّة؟".

كما هو متوقّع، تنتهج الصهيونيّة في مشروعها الاستعماريّ سياسة فرّق تَسُدْ؛ إذ تعمل على تدمير الذاكرة واحتمالات مقاومة السكّان الأصلانيّين الجمعيّة. تقف غزّة في وجه هذه التفرقة بجبهة موحّدة من فصائل المقاومة الفلسطينيّة المتنوّعة، من الإسلاميّة إلى الماركسيّة-اللينينيّة، تحت راية الغرفة المشتركة لفصائل المقاومة. إنّ المقاومة في غزّة هي الأقوى والأكثر ارتكازًا، تعمل بحريّة لا تضاهى في كلّ فلسطين رغم الحصار. تلك هي المعضلة المزدوجة في النضالات المناهضة للاستعمار: هؤلاء الّذين يقاومون هم الأكثر حرّيّة؛ ولذلك، يواجهون أبشع أشكال العنف الاستعماريّ. كما كتب لنا علاء

عبد الفتّاح "غزّة محاصرة لا حبيسة، والفارق شاسع[٥٦]". في هذا الفارق الشاسع، في هذا الحيّز السالب، تتجلّى المقاومة.

لا تكتفي سياسة فرّق تَسُدْ باستهداف وقمع فئات في مجتمعنا بشكل غير متناسق فقط، بل تجعل هذا العنف يبدو بعيدًا واستثنائيًّا. يكمن جوهر استراتيجيّات الاستعمار تحت قناع الاستثنائيّة، وهو عزل غزّة عن فلسطين، وعزل الفلسطينيّين عن العالم، ونزع نضالنا من جذوره، ومنع التوازي السياسيّ وجهود التضامن، وتدمير تاريخ وجود أصحاب الأرض الممتدّ منذ آلاف السّنين. تُسْتَخدم استراتيجيّة الاستثناء لإضفاء الشرعيّة وتبرير الوحشيّة الاستعماريّة، حيث يُعلّق القانون تحت ذريعة حالة الاستثناء لارتكاب الجرائم، والحقيقة هي أنّ العنف يشكّل القاعدة الأساسيّة للاستعمار. تحافظ هذه الاستراتيجيّة على القانون الاستعماريّ تحديدًا من خلال تعليقه، من أجل إدارة العواطف النّابعة من الفكر الليبراليّ وجعل العنف الاستعماريّ يبدو عقلانيًّا ومبرّرًا. في الواقع، لا يتغاضى تعليق القانون فقط عن التجاوزات والانتهاكات الاستعماريّة، بل هو كما وصفه المفكّر القانونيّ الفلسطينيّ وائل حلّاق "إعادة خلق انتهاكات هذه القواعد كقواعد جديدة[٥٧]".

نذكر هنا المثال الأليم لقصف المستشفى المعمداني، والّذي افترض العالم كلّه أنّه استثنائيّ، فلا يعقل أن يكون غير ذلك، لكنّه ما لبث أن تكرّر كمعيار حرب جديد، في مستشفيات الشفاء وكمال عدوان وناصر والإندونيسي، على سبيل المثال لا الحصر. تكمن الخطورة في ترسيخ الوضع الاستثنائيّ لغزّة ليصبح المعتاد بتطبيع حصارها وقصفها المتكرّر، أو بفرض ما يسمّى "حالة الطوارئ" الاستعماريّة عليها، وطرح هذا العنف كمنهجيّات مقبولة للتحكّم بسكّان المناطق المحتلّة، بحسب عقليّة ولغة المستعمِر.

"هل الخوفَ مخيفٌ؟[٥٨]"
أظنّ حَسَب
بس خوفِك أكيد بخوّفني

٥٦
عبد الفتّاح، ٢٠٢١.

٥٧
وائل حلّاق، قصور الاستشراق: منهج في نقد العلم الحداثي، ترجمة عمرو عثمان (بيروت: الشبكة العربية للأبحاث والنشر، ٢٠١٩)، ص ٣٣٣.

٥٨
نعمة حسن، "هكذا نُهَدْهِد الحرب لتنام"، مجلّة الدراسات الفلسطينيّة، العدد ١٣٧ (٢٠٢٤)، ص ٣٢٣.

٦

بغيروا نظرتهم لإلنا بكبسة كبّاسة
عِد للتلاتة
هُبْ
مِن خَطَر لَعَدَمُه
مِن معسكر لمخيّم
مِن فَلَحُه لَعَمَرُه
مِن جماعة لَفَرْد
بِسلاسة
بِدهُم نفقد الأمل
الموضوع مش بس شَماتة
مش لازم نسمّيهم مرضى نفسيّين
هيك بنبرّئ الإنسان من النّجاسة
هُبْ
من اسم قرية لاسم مجزرة
من بشر لَمَبْشَرة
من سكني لأحمرة
ألوان إبادة

تتأرجح إجراءات الحكم الاستعماريّ بين الحياة والموت بشكل خطير، إذ تلغي التمييز بين إدارة السياسة الحيويّة وإدارة الموت. يتمّ توظيف مخيّمات اللاجئين الفلسطينيّة وغيرها من المعازل بوصفها أماكن مهمّشة ومنفيّة كمخازن للعمالة ("معسكرات لليد العاملة") تحت وطأة النظام الصهيونيّ للهيمنة الحيويّة. تكشف المرونة المجدولة لهذه المعازل المهمّشة مدى قابليّة استغناء النظام الاستعماريّ عن حياتهم، وتجريدها من كلّ المقوّمات؛ كما كتب وليد دقّة في عامه الثالث والعشرين من الأسر: "هكذا ليغدو الشعب الفلسطينيّ أقلّ من شعب وفوق الإبادة المادّيّة[٥٩]". مؤكّدًا "كما أنّ معازل الفلسطينيّين ليست جيتوات مؤقّتة ومحطّات يجمعون فيها قبل 'الحلّ النهائيّ'، وإنّما هي *الحلّ النهائيّ*[٦٠]". وأضاف "والمستهدف من هذا الحلّ ليس الجسد عبر إبادة جماعيّة، بل، إن صحّ التعبير، الروح عبر إبادة ثقافيّة وحضاريّة[٦١]".

قد تبدو عبارة وليد دقّة للوهلة الأولى متناقضة مع الإبادة الجماعيّة الحاليّة في غزّة، إلّا أنّها توفّر لنا أدوات لفهم تغيّرات الآليّات الاستعماريّة. إنّ المعازل الفلسطينيّة نفسها هي الحلّ النهائيّ في حدّ ذاته، وعلينا أن نفهم التحوّلات الّتي تفرض بها سيطرتها، وتؤخّر بها الانهيار الوشيك للمستعمرة المتآكلة. نعود بالعبارة الّتي قالها دقّة إلى مفردات النّفي المستعمِرة، فإنّ كلمة *نهائيّ* (من عبارة "الحلّ النهائيّ") مشتقّة من جذر الفعل *[نهى]* الّذي تحدّثنا عنه سابقًا. يعتمد هذا الاشتقاق على تحديد نقطة نهاية، والّذي يمثّل الهدف الاستعماريّ الأساسيّ؛ إنهاء الوجود الفلسطينيّ بالتقييد حتّى الاختناق. فكلّما اتّسع النطاق الاستعماريّ، تقلّصت قطع الأراضي الّتي يتمّ عزل الفلسطينيّين فيها. يمهّد هذا التوسّع الاستعماريّ المتعمّد الانتقال من السيطرة الحيويّة إلى السيطرة المبنيّة على الموت، ممّا يشترط علينا قبول التداخل المشوّه ما بين الحياة والموت.

تعا عالي
ياما ياما مات
بس رجعت و جيت
بأناشيد

٥٩
دقّة، صهر الوعي، ٣٠.

٦٠
دقّة، ٣٢.

٦١
دقّة، ٣٢.

تكمن أهمّيّة طرح دقّة المذكور أعلاه في رفض الانصياع إلى المغالطة الاستعماريّة، إذ تشمل المعازل كلًّا من السلطة الحيويّة والسلطة النكروويّة تحت مبدأ استعماريّ واحد، دافعة بالوجود الفلسطينيّ إلى نهايته. يُعْتَبر استشهاد دقّة في ٧ نيسان ٢٠٢٤، أحد تداعيات هذا التعقيد الاستعماريّ، إذ رُفِض الإفراج عنه مرارًا، بالرغم من أنّه شُخِّص بنوع نادر وعنيف من سرطان نخاع العظام. نرى في هذا تعذيب ممنهج، علاوة على الإهمال الطبّيّ، إذ أدّى تلقّيه الحدّ الأدنى من العلاج بجرعات متباعدة في نهاية الأمر إلى موت بطيء ومؤلم. يجسّد السجن الاستعماريّ، والّذي يمثّل معزلًا فلسطينيًّا "مصغّرًا"، الحدّ النهائيّ للأسرى الفلسطينيّين، حيث تُحْبَس أنفاسهم، وتبقى معلّقة ضمن توازن هشّ. وأخيرًا، يُشكّل الاحتجاز المطوّل والقسريّ لجثمان دقّة في المشارح الاستعماريّة شهادة مروّعة على تلاحم أنظمة القتل والسيطرة الحيويّة، محتجزةً الفلسطينيّين الأسرى أحياء كانوا أم أمواتًا[٦٢].

توفّر لنا تغيّريّة المشروع الاستعماريّ دليلًا على أنّه مشروع غير ثابت؛ وبالتّالي، يمكن تفكيكه حتّى ينهار ماديًّا، وينتهي من الوجود. تطرح عالمة الأنثروبولوجيا والمؤرّخة آن ستولر أنّ "المستعمرة" كمفهوم سياسيّ ليست مكانًا، بل مبدأ لإدارة التنقّلات، تحرّك السكّان وفقًا لقواعد وتسلسلات هرميّة متغيّرة لتنظيم الأنواع الاجتماعيّة: بين من هم مؤهّلون للتجنيد وإعادة التوطين وللإبعاد وللدعم وللعمل القسريّ، وآخرون خارج هذه المعادلة يسْجَنون في معازل[٦٣]". يتبع المعزل الاستعماريّ هذا المبدأ، مقيّدًا الحركة بفرض التصاريح وحظر التنقّل، مجزّئاً السكّان، مجرّداً مَنْ تمّ تجريدهم تاريخيّاً مراراً وتكراراً، وساجنًا ومُعْدِمًا العُصاة. يتبع المعزل منطق المستعمرة في كونه لا مكان، يحوّل الأرض إلى مناطق ومخيّمات وسجون، ويتأرجح في سياساته بين حظر الحياة وإنهائها. المعزل ليس مجرّد تكثيف سكّانيّ في مناطق ضيّقة، بل تقسيم استراتيجيّ للأجساد إلى وحدات قياس سهلة الإدارة والضبط، في حياتها وموتها. وهكذا تُضْهَر الأرض وشعبها لخدمة الأهداف الاستعماريّة، سواء للعمل والإنتاج أو الموت والإبادة.

نرفض التمييز بين إدارة الحياة الّتي تمنحنا فتات الخبز، وإدارة الموت الّتي تفتك بنا وترسله على هيئة صورايخ وقنابل تغزو سماءنا. ولا يتعارض التكوين الليبراليّ لمخيّم اللاجئين كبنية خيريّة لترتيب أمور المهجّرين مع البنية التحتيّة الإمبرياليّة لمعسكرات الاعتقال. كما يقول ناصر أبو رحمة، "هذه الأنواع المختلفة ظاهريًّا ليست نظائر منفصلة، بل أجزاء من كلٍّ واحد[٦٤]". كانت مخيّمات النصيرات والبريج والمغازي في غزّة تحوي مجموعة من المنشآت العقابيّة البريطانيّة الإمبرياليّة مثل النقاط العسكريّة، وثكنات الشرطة، ومراكز الاحتجاز، ومعسكرات الاعتقال، قبل أن تصبح مخيّمات للّاجئين في عام ١٩٤٨. يكشف لنا هذا التاريخ أنّ المعزل ليس حدثًا استثنائيًّا أو عشوائيًّا في ممارسات الاحتلال، بل هو متأصّل في الإمبراطوريّة، ويتحوّل بشكل دوريّ للحفاظ على سلطته. أُعيد تدوير الماضي وما يحويه من آثار للمؤسّسات العقابيّة في المخيّمات والمعازل الفلسطينيّة، وإنتاجه كحاضر ذي طابع خيريّ على صورة مأوى

للّاجئين. تتحوّل الإمبرياليّة ولكنّها لا تختفي، إذ إنّها تقبع في مشاريع الإغاثة والتنمية الإنسانيّة، إذ تحاول الإمبرياليّة اختلاق الوهم التاريخيّ لتبدأ مرحلة ما بعد الاستعمار، بينما تحرق الصهيونيّة المخيّمات الفلسطينيّة. يتجلّى التناقض الزائف بين السياسة الحيويّة للإغاثة الإنسانيّة والسياسة المميتة للإبادة الجماعيّة بشكل خاصّ اليوم في غزّة، حيث تُصْبِح "المناطق الآمنة" أفخاخًا للموت، والحصص الغذائيّة طُعْمًا لسفك دماء الجياع[٦٥]، كما يكون "الرصيف البحري الإنسانيّ" منصّة تشهد على عمليّات القتل، وتصبح شاحنات المساعدات بمثابة حصان طروادة الّذي يمكّن قوّة الاستعمار من ارتكاب المزيد من الفظائع[٦٦].

٦٢
في أثناء فترة سجنه، كتب دقّة مسرحيّة عن وعي الشهيد الفلسطينيّ في الحياة الآخرة، حيث يستيقظ ليجد نفسه محبوسًا في ثلّاجة داخل مشرحة سجن تحت الاحتلال إلى جانب شهداء آخرين. تعكس المسرحيّة تشابهًا مؤلمًا مع حالة دقّة بعد وفاته، مسلّطة الضوء على انتشار هذه الجريمة الاستعماريّة المروّعة. دقّة، "الشهداء يعودون إلى رام الله" (أرشيف مخطوطات وليد دقّة، ٢٠٢١). لمناقشة متعمّقة حول المسرحيّة، راجعوا مقالة عبد الرحيم الشيخ الّتي تحمل العنوان نفسه في مجلّة الدراسات الفلسطينيّة، العدد ١٣٣ (٢٠٢٣): ١٢٨-١٥٥.

٦٣
آن ستولر، الإكراه: دراسة عن المتانة الإمبراطوريّة في العصر الحديث [Duress: Imperial Durabilities in Our Times] (دورهام: دار نشر جامعة ديوك، ٢٠١٦)، ١١٧.

٦٤
ناصر أبو رحمة، ٢٧٩.

٦٥
في إشارة إلى مجزرة الطحين غرب مدينة غزّة في ٢٩ شباط ٢٠٢٤، عندما أطلقت القوّات الاستعماريّة الصهيونيّة النار على فلسطينيّين جائعين كانوا ينتظرون قوافل المساعدات، ممّا أسفر عن مقتل ١١٨ شخصًا وإصابة ٧٦٠ آخرين.

٦٦
بخصوص مجزرة ٧ تمّوز ٢٠٢٤ في مخيّم النصيرات للّاجئين في غزّة، عندما تسلّل الجنود الصهاينة إلى المخيّم عن طريق الاختباء في قافلة مساعدات، ثمّ فتحوا النار على الفلسطينيّين النازحين قبل أن يشنّوا غارات جوّيّة على المخيّم، ممّا أسفر عن مقتل ما لا يقلّ عن ٢٧٦ فلسطينيًّا وإصابة حوالي ٧٠٠ آخرين. تمّ تسهيل هذه المجزرة بتورّط الولايات المتّحدة، بما في ذلك دعمها الاستخباراتيّ واستخدامها الخسيس لرصيف توصيل المساعدات الإنسانيّة المموّل من بايدن—وهو فعل يتماشى كلّيًّا مع سياسة الولايات المتّحدة الخارجيّة الإمبرياليّة. لم يتفاجأ الفلسطينيّون من إعلان الولايات المتّحدة عن تفكيك هذا الرصيف بعد وقت قصير من المجزرة، الذي كشف بوضوح عن النيّة العنيفة وراء إنشائه.

بتحكي مع حالك وَلا
بلا لَف ودوران بلا بطّيخ
بَعْمَل مِن عينيك دَوا
علّم عالطّبّاخ طّبّيخ
يا بو مليون كذبة
والمساعدات أَوْسَخْها
كل الشّعب آفْرَك
زيّك زي القَبْلَك، فِش أرجى

إنّ الانتقال من الحياة إلى الموت، ومن الأرض إلى السجن، ومن الشعب إلى السكّان، ومن المقاومة إلى الشهادة، يُبرز الطبيعيّة المتغلغلة والهشّة لهذا النّفي الاستعماريّ، إذ تطفو المستعمرة بشكل غير مستقرّ على الحافّة، فمن الممكن استعادة الأرض، تمامًا كما تمّ تقليصها إلى منطقة. أظهرت المقاومة الفلسطينيّة مرارًا وتكرارًا قابليّة اختراق الحدود الاستعماريّة ذات التوسّع المستمرّ والجشع اللامحدود للأرض، ممّا جعلها عرضة للفشل. أكّد محمود العارضة، أحد الأسرى الستّة الّذين حفروا طريقهم عبر الأنفاق للخروج من سجن جلبوع، على زوال المشروع الاستعماريّ الصهيونيّ وقرب عودة الفلسطينيّين، عندما صرّح: "أردنا أن نقول للأمّة إنّ هذا الوحش وهم من غبار". كلمات عارضة في المحكمة لا تُقلّل من الثّقل البنيويّ للاستعمار، والّذي تعرّض له شخصيًّا بالهجوم والضّرب من قبل ضبّاط الاحتلال، بل هو تعبير عن رفضه القاطع لأن يسحق تحت وطأته. يدعونا هذا الواقع للتفكير، بأنّ أولئك الّذين يتواجدون في الحيّز السالب، المنفيّون والمتأرجحون على حافّة الموت، هم الأكثر إيمانًا بالحياة والتحرير.

في صلب الشعار الصهيونيّ "أرض بلا شعب لشعب بلا أرض" إصرار على فرض فراغ خطابيّ، وبالرغم من ذلك، فقد فشلت الصهيونيّة في تحقيق هذا الفراغ. في هذه الأرض الّتي أسقط عليها الحكم اللغويّ بأنّها بلا شعب، تفيض الحياة الأصلانيّة دائمًا ضدّ مخطوطات الاستعمار، وتتسرّب خارج حدوده مواجِهةً لشطبٍ وإعادة احتواء وخنق دائمين. يظهر غيابنا في البيوت المكدّسة فوق الدونمات المكلفة المتآكلة، وعلى طوابير الحواجز، وفي السجون المكتظّة، وفي مواكب الحداد والعودة، وفي معدّلات الولادة المرتفعة الّتي تشير إليها الصّهيونية وهي تبيد عائلات بأكملها. حتمًا، تزداد شدّة القمع في المعزل يومًا بعد يوم. مع ذلك، يتمّ تحطيم هذا المعزل، تحفر فيه الأنفاق، يُحَلَّق فوقه، ويفكّك تمامًا. كم كان سلسًا انهيار المستوطنات في غزّة وجنين، حين تحوّل ثقلها البنيويّ إلى غبار[٦٧]، كأنّهم لم يكونوا.

كلهم مستعمرين، من بيت إيل لتل أبيب اصحكم تصدقوهم. والله مصيرهم رحيل وأنا بغنّي من روحي. آه هم حياخدوا روحي؟

يؤدّي عجز المشروع الاستعماريّ عن جعل هذه الأرض بلا شعب، إلى تفكّك ترابط عناصر استقراره، ممّا يخلق مساحة لصنع واقع آخر. تقاوم الأرض إفراغها، وتنبثق منها الحياة الأصلانيّة في مواجهة القوى الدخيلة، متجاوزة الحدود الخرائطيّة الاستعماريّة لتشهد على أنقاض القرى المدمّرة، تخليدًا لذكرى عدد لا يحصى من شهدائنا الّذين لا ولن نعرفهم. لم يكتمل تحميض صورتنا السالبة بعد، ولكنّ حضورنا الغائب سيعلن الحياة، وقريبًا، سيحلّ الدّفء على الأرجوانيّ وتحمرّ التربة[٦٨]. ننتظر عودة عمّالنا من نطاق مستعبِديهم وأسرانا من سجّانيهم، نحيك الجغرافيّات الخمس معًا وندمّر السادسة، متحرّرين نتنصّل ذاتنا من سلبها لتعود إلى الأرض.

٦٧
هذا لا يعني التقليل من حجم الركّام والنفايات الّتي ألقيت على الأراضي الفلسطينيّة المحرّرة. فبعد انتصار المقاومة في عام ٢٠٠٥، قامت الجرّافات الصهيونيّة بتدمير جميع المواقع العسكريّة والمستوطنات الّتي كانت تعجّ بها غزّة لمنع الفلسطينيّين من استخدامها، تاركة وراءها الفساد الاستعماريّ والأنقاض كنوع من الانتقام لتحرير غزّة. (ومع ذلك، كما نعلم، جاء الانتقام الأساسيّ على شكل الحصار). للمزيد حول بقايا الإمبراطوريّة السامّة، انظروا مقدّمة آن ستولر في المجلّد المحرّر الذي أشرفت عليه بعنوان "بقايا الإمبراطوريّة: حول الأنقاض والخراب" [Imperial Debris: On Ruins and Ruination] (دورهام: دار نشر جامعة ديوك، ٢٠١٣)، الصفحات ١-٣٥.

٦٨
باسل عبّاس وروان أبو رحمة، ليت النسيان، -٢٠٢١.

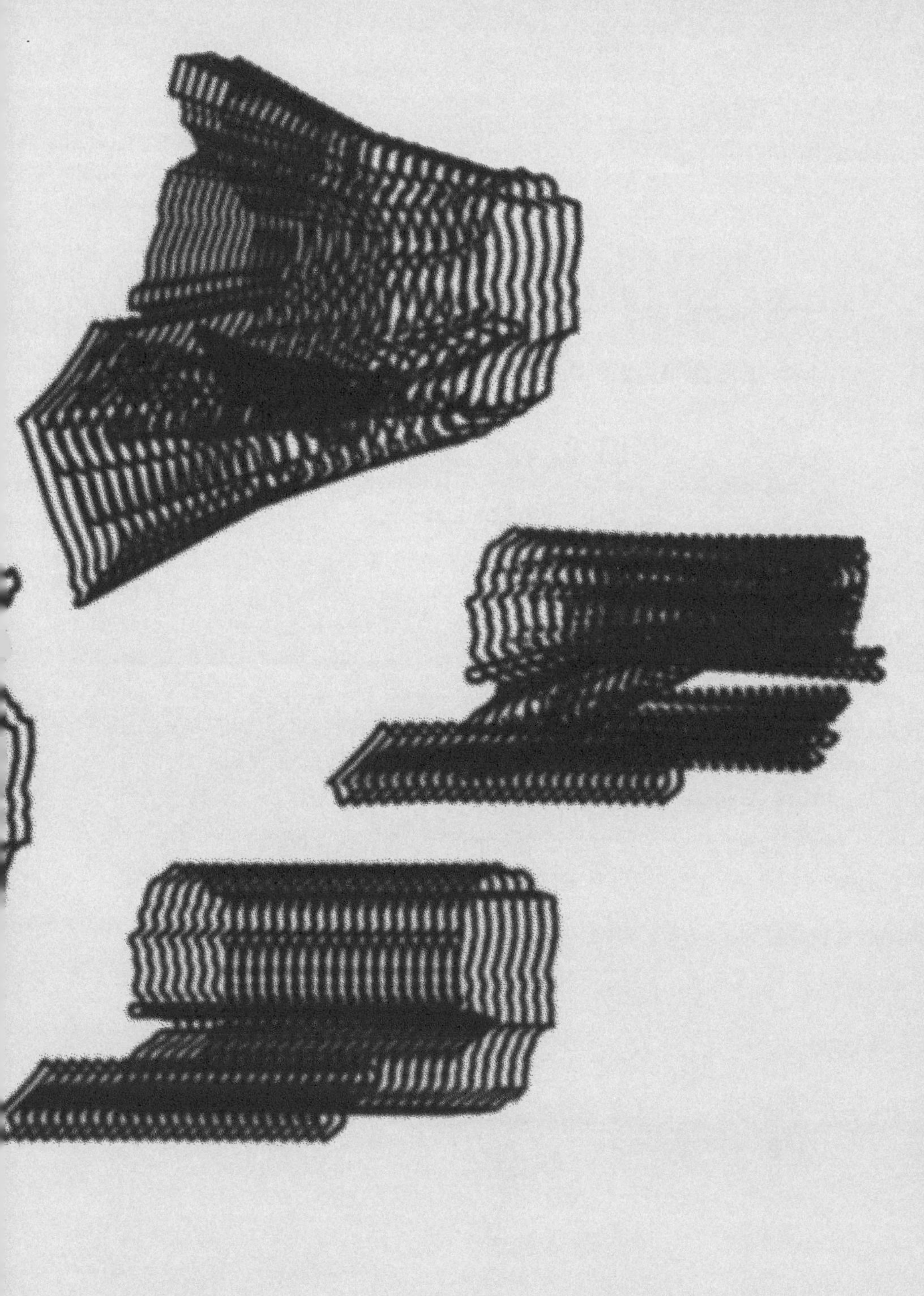